Contents

Preface

Whatever you do will be insignificant, but it is very important that you do it. *Mahatma Ghandi*

This book outlines training ideas and principles for the committed *aikidoka* (Aikido artist). It is hoped that the various ideas and principles will give the reader the means to map out a personal strategy for dissecting Aikido into its parts and reconstructing those ideas to create new knowledge. Then, keeping those ideas in mind, the *aikidoka* should be able to apply it to his own Aikido practice.

Many of the principles also relate to other martial arts. Students of all martial arts should be aware that each art requires its own physical attributes. Aikido practice concentrates on numerous joint locks and heavy throws, so, for reasons of safety, it is imperative for participants to consult a doctor if they have any doubts about their physical capability. Furthermore, since many people start a martial art to increase their confidence and ability in self-defence, it is important to understand the legal ramifications of any action. For a brief explanation on self-defence and the law, *see* Appendix III.

For Aikido beginners or those who practise other arts, a brief introduction of Aikido terminology and training practices is necessary. Aikido is commonly referred to as 'The Way of Harmony'. Just as a *judoka* practises Judo, so an *aikidoka* practises Aikido. Japanese terminology is italicized and is further explained in the glossary of terms (*see* page 172). The *dojo* (training hall) is the training venue and *tatami* (training mats) are used to make life easier. The *sensei* (teacher) sits at the far wall opposite the door and the students line up facing him. Out of respect, teacher and students *rei* (bow) first to a picture of O Sensei (Ueshiba Morihei, the founder of Aikido) and then to each other at the beginning and end of class. Students also *rei* to each other every time they change training partners.

The attacker is called *uke* (receiver of applied technique) and the defender is called *tori* (the do-er). When *uke* falls, he is said to take *ukemi* (break-fall).

Aikido techniques are done from three positions: *tachi-waza* (standing), *suwari-waza* (kneeling), and *hanmi-handachi* (one standing and one kneeling). Three weapons are incorporated into Aikido training: *bokken* (sword), *jo* (staff) and *tanto* (knife).

Two main principles of Aikido are *irimi* (entering) and *tenkan* (turning). Sometimes called *omote* and *ura*, these two principles usually dictate the training routine. The idea of *irimi* is to enter *uke*'s attack and to cross *uke*'s front. It is quite a difficult concept to comprehend and might be likened to entering the attack with the intent of reversing it back upon *uke*. Contrasting this, when performing *tenkan*, *tori* turns, moves to the rear, and allows *uke*'s attack to continue in its intended direction. Typically, *uke* attacks *tori* four

4

times, alternating left and right. The first two times *tori* performs two *irimi* techniques, typically one from right posture, and then another from the left. The second two times, *tori* performs two *tenkan* techniques, again, from both the left and the right. After that, the roles are reversed.

In Aikido, the role of *uke*, the receiver, is often considered to be equal in importance to that of *tori* (if not more important), since being controlled or thrown offers insight into how the techniques are performed.

Aikido movement can broadly be divided into three types:

• basic exercises train the body to move in a predetermined way;
• *kokyu-ho* (breath exercise) and *kokyu-nage* (breath throw) are midway between exercise and technique and consist of simple movements that help *tori* to harmonize with and move *uke* in efficient manner;
• Aikido *waza* (techniques) consist of immobilizations, where *uke* is directed to the floor and held down, and projections, where *uke* is thrown.

The technical aim of Aikido is not just to learn a vast array of *waza*. Rather, the *aikidoka* should aim to perfect a limited number of techniques. It is important to internalize what is learned in the basic exercises and *kokyu* practice and incorporate it all into the *waza*; this is easy to say, but very difficult to do. With time, the *aikidoka* will become aware of endless variations as the principles of Aikido become more apparent. Unfortunately, many never get this far, which is why I hope this book should be useful.

Introduction

I started out with nothing and I still have most of it left.
Anon

The Japanese art of Aikido is commonly referred to as 'The Way of Harmony'. On closer analysis, the word is often split up into its constituent parts with the explanation that *Ai* translates as 'union', *ki* as 'energy', and *do* as 'path'. *Aiki* may also be interpreted as a single component that represents the meeting and flow of liquid energy between training partners. It is not easy to fathom from words alone, but a number of ideas and concepts should help the keen student to come to a better understanding.

The principle of *aiki* is what the student of the art should be seeking. It is not that other arts do not have it, but Aikido chooses to name it, and aims to develop it. Occasionally, practitioners of other arts appear to have it, yet do not know they have it; as a consequence, they have no means of easily passing it on. Therefore, it is apparent that *aiki* can be acquired with no knowledge through extensive practice. Furthermore, those who have training in *aiki* tend to learn other arts more rapidly; many of the arts contain similar principles, even though they may not be specifically targeted in training.

Any martial art requires an understanding of the value of co-ordination, space and time. Co-ordination is acquired by physically going through the motions with a partner. Doing this allows the practitioner to become accustomed to the concept of spatial distance – where he is in relation to his partner and his surroundings – and to the idea of time, or rhythm. In martial arts, and especially in Aikido, some people believe that simply by practising it for ten or twenty years they will somehow acquire 'it', yet they are never quite sure exactly what 'it' is. This cannot be right. Only by thinking about what you are learning can you progress efficiently. Identifying what you need to achieve will help you determine the direction of your study. And identifying what you have achieved will determine whether or not that direction was correct. The person who needs to know this is the self. A beginner should seek the best teachers but along the Way he must become an independent learner. It is only in this way that he will ever out-evolve his teacher, which should, of course, be the greatest compliment. Before you start your journey, you must seek a good club – the one with the best students.

1 Searching

I hear and I forget. I see and I remember. I do and I understand. *Confucius*

Following only one impairs the vision; seeing too many too soon will confuse the mind. In time, it is not hard to tell who is, and who is not, a good teacher.

Finding One to Follow

The Master will doddle along, delegate authority, provide occasional words of wisdom, often smile, and, on occasion, might even demonstrate a technique. He is only really qualified when he is of a certain age, in light of a lifetime of experience; he may be an older student who still participates in the activities but has nothing to prove. Respect will come naturally but is of no great concern; what has been learned will never be forgotten. The would-be Master is the one who fulfils the above criteria but lacks experience. He may be eager to be thought of as Master, seeking nothing but recognition, when he should be seeking only the Way. He may ask others to perform that which he was never able to do himself. Respect has to be explained and then enforced, and is only given to those who have something he wants.

The Teacher imparts wisdom to the seeking student, inspires the student to learn through little more than good example, and is not much more than a guide or single point of reference in the subsequent development. Respect is natural. The would-be Teacher comes with much theory and doctrine and is always eager to point out detailed technicality to demonstrate his knowledge, but what he knows deteriorates in time as he no longer trains. Respect is another technique and is thoroughly explained, as well as being compulsory. Respect is given to whoever praises him.

The Student is the seeker, has a hunger for knowledge, and aims to be the best he can. Respect comes naturally. The would-be Student is the one who wants the knowledge but is not prepared to do the work. He can often be found explaining everything to his fellow students or absorbed in some obscure religious doctrine, oblivious to reality. Respect is given to anyone who will listen.

Finding the Path

In the beginning, the student has no idea what Aikido is, let alone what he should seek. Worse still, as he advances he may not even realize that he should be seeking, and come to depend on and trust completely in his teacher, believing that such association will somehow rub off. A passive learner will never evolve to the extent of an active seeker. Therefore, it is important for the beginning student to know that it is he himself who will be responsible for the major part of his journey. Of course, having a great teacher is the best way to start, but a beginner has no certain way of discerning what a good teacher is.

Accordingly, the smart beginner will need to develop a discerning eye; seeing as many teachers as possible gives a basis for comparison, but not a guarantee.

Concrete objectives need to be set, for example, improving health and stamina, becoming more co-ordinated, learning basic movements, understanding space and time, achieving a few grades, increasing overall confidence, gaining competence in self-defence, and so on. You also need to establish the means to achieve these objectives. The factor that binds all these together to create Aikido is *aiki*. Maintaining his aims in relation to *aiki* from early on will keep the student in correct focus.

The student should not expect sudden enlightenment; rather, the journey will be a collection of successive mini-enlightenments as things slowly click into place. In the beginning, the learning curve is fast. Later, months will pass with seemingly little improvement, then, suddenly, something will be realized, a jump will be made up to the next level, and everything changes. It is a process that repeats itself endlessly, rewarding only those who show patience.

The ideas explored here are intended to help those seeking the Way to know where they are and to keep focus on where they are going.

OPPOSITE: Find direction and move ahead.

2 Etiquette

Intense love does not measure; it just gives.
Mother Teresa

If there is one thing, more than any other, that is common between the fighting systems of the world, it is etiquette. Importance is placed on respecting the training partner, the competitor, and even the enemy. And by respecting the other, one benefits the self; exercises in etiquette represent the more human element of the fighting arts and the emphasis usually carries over into the character of the practitioner in daily life.

The *Dojo*
Tatami
Full-time *dojo*s are a rare sight in the West. Accordingly, laying the *tatami* (mats) is an important pre-class ritual. Everyone should be involved with laying the *tatami* and those who regularly arrive too late or leave early will be viewed with a certain amount of unspoken scorn.

There are several kinds of *tatami* and each school has its own peculiar method of laying them down. Judo *tatami* are the most expensive and regarded as the best. Some mix red and green randomly, others carefully create patterns, most use just green. A second popular type is the canvas laid over foam *tatami*. The canvas is secured using wooden beams that surround the *tatami*, being held together with a piece of rope that threads its way between the canvas cover and screws poking out of the wooden beams. The last choice are jigsaw mats, which are thin and cheap, and come in every colour.

Cleaning the Dojo
If students are fortunate enough to train in a *dojo* with a permanent *tatami*, they are usually required to sweep it before and after training. In some *dojo*s, it is even required to clean the windows. Often, the *dojo* is not even dirty, but the ritual must be carried out nevertheless in order to instil a necessary air of humility in the trainees. If classes run back to back, then it is usual just to clean up after training, not before.

Procedure
Lining Up
When lining up at the beginning of the class the students should make a straight line according to the person to their immediate right. Traditionally, but not always in Aikido, the seniors, or *sempai*, sit to the right. If this is the case, the line should run from wherever the senior sits; either way, it should always run from the person who is sitting to the far right. If the line is not straight – for example, if the senior student, or part of the line, is sitting slightly forwards or backwards – then something is wrong. A beginner at the lower end of the line can do nothing, however, except match his position to that of the person to the immediate right. He must not become

out of place by matching his position to that of a senior further up the line. If the problem is halfway along the line, that is where the correction needs to be; subsequent shuffling down the line will lead to the line becoming straight. With children, starting a class without that straight line is the surest way to chaos.

Bowing

When bowing from a kneeling position, the body necessarily bends at the waist and the student places first the left then the right palm on the *tatami*. It is not good form for the backside to rise as the head lowers. In a standing position the body should bend not at the waist, but a little higher, around the solar plexus region; in martial arts, the bow should not be too deep. One bow should equal one breath, and the bow should be neither too quick nor too slow, just deliberate. You should always look up slightly towards your partner, and if the school dictates that you look down then you should try to be as aware as possible of where others are and what they are doing. The emphasis is on awareness, not on looking. The act is one of both courtesy and trust – your martial awareness is ready, in case that trust be broken. Practitioners should bow at the beginning when meeting a new partner, and at the end. There is no need to bow every time the *tori* and *uke* roles are swapped. Excessive bowing or contests in humility are unnecessary.

When bowing to a partner, it is best for both to bow at the same time, in harmony. Otherwise, it is up to the junior student to match the time of the senior. If the teacher appears during training and helps with the technique it is customary to thank them with a bow. However, some teachers do not like it if students repeatedly prostrate themselves at this time, since it may make them feel as though they have to respond in a similar fashion. The student should be aware that, by performing a kneeling bow, they are forcing their teacher to do the same, making them feel awkward if they do not do so. Instead, the student should take the lead of the teacher. If the teacher goes down for a kneeling bow, the student should follow. A short standing bow will often suffice, though, as long as it is equal to, or a little deeper than that of the teacher. The student should bow at exactly the same time, but aim to come up just a moment later.

Japanese university freshmen bow while saying the phrase '*onegaeshimas*', meaning 'Please train with me'. As they near graduation, that phrase finds itself reduced to something like the '*oossu*' often heard in Karate *dojo*s.

Talking

Chatting while training is bad form. Telling your partner what to do while training is bad form. When your partner is obviously stuck, try leading them through the technique without words – be a pliable *uke*. If you must speak, it should be limited to telling your partner which posture to start in. Give him every chance to figure it out for himself. Otherwise, sit down, watch someone else, and then try again.

Another problem is that some teachers talk too much. If you do not like it, and many do not, all you can really do about it is learn the lesson and not talk too much when you become a teacher.

Ego

The ego is named as the obstacle to be overcome. This is an ideal philosophy suited to opulent Lords of the past who demanded subservience from their vassals, yet it often appears in devious form in the very place that is supposed to squash it:

the *dojo* often reflects it, being full of those who seek favour with flattery or exaggerated attention. Not easy to remove, but easy to see. Excessive bowing or politeness can be one form. Learn from the examples displayed before you every day. It makes quite interesting study.

Leaving the tatami

With good preparation, the student should never have to leave the *tatami* during training. Many consider it as a kind of failure. If you have eaten too much and feel sick then you have failed your self. If you have not eaten all day and feel queasy, then you have failed your self. If you forget to go to the bathroom before the session and have to leave the *tatami*, you lose training time, and have failed your self. If you forget to take your watch or ring off, you have failed yourself. If you forget to cut your nails, you fail your self. If you need a drink of water midway, you fail your self, even if it is allowed (if the training is hard, some clubs have a scheduled break for the students to replenish themselves with a little water).

However, if you do need to leave the *tatami* for any reason, you should simply do so, even if the teacher seems to be annoyed. If the teacher is angry, view it as their own personal problem, not yours. You do not need to give a reason, but it is polite to inform the teacher that you are leaving the *tatami* since he needs to know where all the students are. Training is a chance to practise overcoming adversity and a significant part of the battle is in preparation.

Etiquette as Art

Some say that Judo is 90 per cent etiquette. I failed to understand this for years until I saw an old movie clip of Kano Jigoro, the founder of Judo, performing a few techniques. It was Judo *kata* (form) demonstrated to perfection, suggesting that Judo is in the *kata*, not in the *shiai* (competition). It was not a fight, but a perfect dynamic demonstration of Judo principles. Perhaps Aikido too, is 90 per cent etiquette.

3 Warming Up

All difficult things have their origin in that which is easy, and great things in that which is small. *Lao Tzu*

If there is no sweat there is no heat. Warming up the body prepares it for stretching the limbs, which in turn prepares it for safe work. If the preparation programme is well designed, it also prepares the mind for Aikido.

Preparation

Do not eat a large meal before training. Indeed, you should not consume anything at all, except a small drink, fewer than thirty minutes before the class is due to begin. Hard training or a sudden shock can cause you to feel or be sick. Also, try to go to the bathroom before class begins.

On approaching the *dojo*, you will typically begin to think about Aikido. The posture straightens and you may feel your limbs automatically stretch in anticipation. Avoidance movements and techniques may flash through the mind. The breathing is regulated and the mind becomes more alert.

The modern tradition dictates that students typically train in the evenings, at the end of the school or working day. Instead, try training in the morning as a preparation for the whole day. If no Aikido class is available, you can warm up with lots of *aiki* exercises for half an hour, and, if you have the time, run through a few techniques on your own with an imaginary partner. This is excellent preparation for the day – a kind of physical and spiritual breakfast.

Warm-up exercises, whether at home or in the *dojo*, should all be martial in nature and related to Aikido. Breathing, postures, footwork, *taisabaki*, *torifune* and *ukemi* all prepare the body for training, both spiritually and mentally. Whether doing a gentle or vigorous warm-up, make sure that your breathing matches the movements. Concentrating on breathing in rhythm to movement in the warm-up exercises will eventually, naturally, transfer over to the techniques. However, beginners need to engage in a certain amount of conscious thinking to get the process started; after this, it is often best to forget about it and let it happen naturally.

The Basics

Everyone knows that students have to practise the basics, or *kihon*, but what does this really mean? *Kihon* usually refers to postural, footwork, or avoidance exercises done just after the warm-up. Most *dojos* seem happy to get them out of the way as soon as possible. However, the truth seems to be that it is not until you begin to find the basics interesting that you really begin to learn. Furthermore, the *dojo* environment is often not conducive to *kihon* practice. It is better to go over the basics elsewhere in your own time until they feel right; by the time you think they are 'right', they will have become interesting. Soon you will find new minor variations that can ultimately reveal themselves in modified techniques; and just when you have finally understood, you discover something else new – it is an endless process of self-discovery.

In many *dojo*s, it seems that what is learned in the basics does not show itself in the techniques. Do not fall into this trap. If your basic training is not useful in your techniques then you are almost certainly barking up the wrong tree. It goes without saying that you need to practise basic movements with repetitive vigour until they become ingrained in muscle and sinew memory.

Flexibility

Flexibility is important for safety and for health. Training for flexibility should never be done until the body is warm as injury could result. The older the person, the longer the warm-up and the gentler the stretching should be. When training slowly and gently you can work at the extremities of flexibility. In Karate, for example, working at the limit might mean slowly stretching a kick to head height. When training with more speed and power you should stay well away from the extremities, otherwise you may be inviting injury. A *Karateka* adding power to a sidekick at his limit is more likely to hurt himself than his opponent.

Obviously, the more flexible you are, the more range you have within which to work and the safer your practice will be. Gentle flexibility exercises in co-ordination with breathing also help you to relax, perhaps leading to a more flexible mind. The main rule of thumb is to stretch and hold, not bounce. Bouncing at your extremity causes the muscle to contract involuntarily, which is the opposite of what is desired.

Warm-Up Exercises

Twisting the Limbs

There seem to be hundreds of techniques. One way to rationalize the mess is to forget their names and to look at the shapes the body makes. If you extend the arm out forwards, it twists in only two directions – inside and outside. Bringing the wrist close to the chest, twisting it inwards produces *nikyo*, twisting it outwards produces *kote-gaeshi*. When extending the arm outwards, turning it inwards produces a twist similar to *sankyo*, twisting it outwards produces a twist similar to *shiho-nage*. So, here are four techniques with four tricky names that boil down to twisting the arm or wrist in or out, far or near, and much of Aikido is based on these twists, which is why they are included in most warm-up routines.

The legs also twist in and out, and looking at, or feeling, what happens as you twist your legs gently to their extremities will offer an insight into how to move in Aikido.

One typical warm-up exercise is *tenkan-ho*, or turning by yourself or with a partner. Doing it by yourself, you can feel the legs being twisted naturally, perhaps by pivoting, placing all the weight on the front foot. The smart learner will also turn in the opposite direction; this is often not seen in an Aikido class, but such movement exists within many of the techniques and practising it will lead to better understanding. These turning exercises can also be performed with a *bokken* or *jo* (*see* Chapter 17), adding further insight.

'Aiki Yoga'

As a warm-up, partners can perform techniques in a *kokyu-ho* manner. What this means is that *tori* takes control of *uke* as in, say, *tenchi-nage*, but does not throw. Instead, *uke* is stretched over to the rear and holds that position for five to ten

Nikyo twist.

Kote-gaeshi twist.

Sankyo twist.

Shiho-nage twist.

seconds. *Tori* does not support *uke*, nor does *uke* hang from *tori*'s grip, rather, *uke* simply maintains his position making a slight effort to raise up. In another example, *tori* takes *ikkyo* and stops midway, giving *uke* a pleasant stretch that is held for some time, or until *uke* signals *tori* to stop, by tapping.

When practising like this, emphasis should be placed on being slow and careful. Thought is given both to posture and to matching breathing with movement. Here, *tori* and *uke* both benefit at the same time.

Torifune

This stand-up 'rowing the boat' exercise is unique to Aikido. Its purpose is to train the practitioner to push forwards and draw backwards strongly, using the body, not the arms, thereby developing the feeling of moving from the centre. (Note the use of the word 'draw' as opposed to 'pull'; Aikido people often dislike the word 'pull', associating it with excessive use of arm strength.)

While performing *torifune* some people lean slightly forwards and slightly backwards, aligning the spine with the front or rear legs while moving to and fro. Others just stay perpendicular. The method of *torifune* will be apparent in the techniques these people perform, if not, it makes no sense. Both have merit since there are times when performing techniques when a slightly forward-leaning posture is useful; at other times it is more efficient to be straight. Clearly, if what is being done in *torifune* is not reflected in the technique then something is wrong.

Other *kokyu* exercises can also be included in the warm-up.

4 Posture

It is even harder for the average ape to believe that he has descended from man. *H.L. Mencken*

Posture provides the basis of technical structure in Aikido. Each school varies slightly in hand/foot positions, but all stress the importance. Only once posture is understood can the practitioner begin to experiment with no-posture. The following provides a structural look at various positions.

Kneeling

In Japan, it is customary for men to sit with the knees apart, while women are expected to keep the knees together. The best way to generate power in *suwari-waza* (kneeling position) is to have the knees apart, so women should observe Japanese custom for polite sitting only, and utilize the more efficient knees-apart position for practice. When sitting, the back should be straight, the chin back and pressed up, rearwards. On rising, movement should begin from the body's centre, so that the head will up rise at the same time, vertically. Many people begin to rise by moving their shoulders forwards, but this is incorrect.

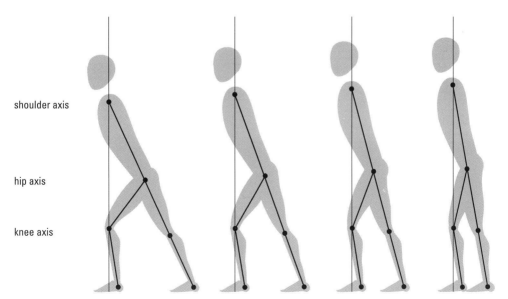

shoulder axis

hip axis

knee axis

The above depict the absolute forward limit of Aikido posture. Aikido movement occurs with the shoulder axis operating somewhere between the knee and hip axes.

When knee-walking, you should make an effort to maintain correct posture. If performing rolls from *suwari-waza*, you should become upright, showing awareness, after each roll. One method to help develop a firmer seated posture is for *uke* to stand behind and gently push *tori*'s shoulders or head in all directions. Everything that is learned in this practice, internally, should be maintained when standing up.

Standing

When standing, the back should be straight, the chin back, and pressed up, rearwards; it is no different from *suwari-waza* or when holding a *bokken* or *jo*. This feeling is not unlike the sensation of wearing a collar and tie that is too tight, which forces the wearer to retract the trachea, to avoid contact with the material. The hips hang neutrally, neither extended too far forwards (or up), nor too far back (or down).

The same guidelines should be followed when moving. When performing technique, the hips should be rotated forwards (or up) at, or just before, the moment of contact, with the feeling that the *hara*, or centre, is extending out to touch *uke*. This is very important and the odds are that it will rarely be corrected.

Upright posture.

Positions

Hanmi/Kamae

Hanmi means 'half posture' and represents what *tori* shows to *uke* – half his posture, which is considered to be less of a target. *Kamae* refers literally to 'posture' but is taken by some schools to mean 'full posture', where the hips are 'square on', facing *uke*. In this stance, if the arms are extended out forwards, the tips of the fingers reach the same point. The main difference may be interpreted as being dependent upon foot positioning.

In both types of posture, the rear leg is typically straight. Weight distribution over the front and rear legs in *hanmi* is typically 70/30 or 60/40 respectively. In *kamae* it is anything from 70/30 to 100/0. In *hanmi* the weight is more centralized, allowing the practitioner to be more flexible, and able to give (by pushing from the rear leg) and take (withdrawing by pushing from the front leg) more freely. In *kamae* the weight is further forward; the rationale says that, since you turn on one leg, you can turn faster because you are already

Hanmi.

Kamae.

there. Of course, in static stances it is easy to make such distinctions, but when moving these two types merge.

Starting Positions
Whether in *hanmi* or *kamae*, it is possible to adopt a high, middle or lower attitude, respectively, *jodan*, *chudan* or *gedan*. In *hanmi*, the front hand extends forward about two hand-lengths ahead of the rear hand. In *kamae*, both hands extend

equally. For standard posture, both *tori* and *uke* begin with one hand in *chudan* and the other in *gedan*, as if holding a sword. The fingers are always splayed open and, even when grabbing *uke*'s arm, you typically hold with the two little fingers and half the middle finger, leaving the index finger open. This may be called the *yonkyo* grip, since it resembles that technique, and can also be used when holding a *bokken* or *jo*.

Jodan.

Chudan.

Gedan.

Meeting Positions

Holding your right arm out, you can meet *uke* in four tactically different positions. First, your right arm can be on the outside of *uke*'s right arm; second, it can be just on the inside; third, your left hand can be on the outside of *uke*'s right arm; and fourth, it can be on the inside. With two arms, then, there are eight possible shapes. This could be systemized in terms of eight attacks, eight avoidances, eight grabs, eight techniques, and so on. Maybe you would require two techniques per position, totalling sixteen.

The same is true for the feet. Judo names the four techniques that match those positions, moving from right to left in like manner, as *O soto-gari*, *ko uchi-gari*, *ko soto-gari* and *O uchi-gari*. The way you meet *uke* in terms of these positions determines which techniques in your repertoire will be called upon. Giving techniques names often complicates simple structural principles.

Ai-hanmi outside.

Ai-hanmi inside.

Gyaku-hanmi outside.

Gyaku-hanmi inside.

Foot Positions

The feet in Aikido typically form the shape of a bow and arrow on the floor, positioned at an angle of some 90-plus degrees to each other. Some schools insist that the front foot must point straight forward all the time. Others insist that the front foot should be turned out as much as possible, enabling the student to utilize his full range of movement. Some place the heels along an imaginary straight line, others dissect the line with the mid-sections of their feet. Others have no firm rules at all. One important commonality, however, is that no Aikido school teaches students to turn the front foot inwards – although many a high-grade instructor can be seen doing this from time to time. Another

important commonality is that, by necessity, those schools that insist on *hanmi* tend to have the front foot pointing forward whereas those who prefer *kamae* turn the foot out.

Interestingly, if you start in *hanmi* with the front foot pointing forwards, and take a step forwards, you will turn the front foot outwards, since it is soon going to become the rear foot. At this point, the hips momentarily become 'square on'. This suggests that, rather being different postures, the foot positions are actually distinct points along a single Aikido postural continuum. Therefore, any argument about why this or that posture is better can really only confirm that neither side of the argument knows the true answer.

21

Hanmi.

Kamae.

Hanmi.

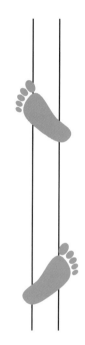

Kamae.

Walking

Ayumi-ashi and *tsugi-ashi* refer respectively to walking step and shuffling (or boxer) step. In Aikido, large forward or diagonal movements are made; in Judo they are much smaller and more shuffling in nature – slower and more cautious. It is important to practise various steps in different directions, varying the speed and power of movement while maintaining posture and awareness. However, you should keep in mind that it is only really through doing the techniques that you can learn the meaning of the movement. Over time, what you practise in the warm-up will become the same as what you are doing in the techniques.

Knee-walking, or *shikko*, isolates wobbly legs from the postural equation and, in the long run, contributes to improved stability when standing up. When performing *shikko*, you should move with the heels together, as though they are tied. When the knee nears the ground, visualize it being the power fulcrum of the technique; even when walking backwards, make positive powerful steps. *Ayumi-ashi*, *tsugi-ashi*, *tais-abaki* and *tenkan* are all possible in *shikko*.

Movement

There are many martial arts and each has its own way of placing the feet on the ground and moving. In a wrestling-based art, such as Judo, the martial artist might tend to have the feet turned out, ball and heel planted firmly on the ground. In a faster-moving art such as Kendo, the feet typically point forwards, with the weight

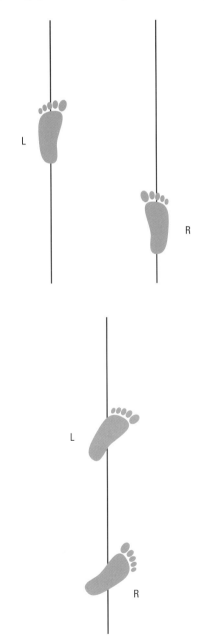

ABOVE: Judo.

TOP RIGHT: Kendo.

BOTTOM RIGHT: Karate.

on the balls of the feet. A horse has four gaits – walk, trot, canter and gallop – so it is puzzling to consider that certain arts limit humans to one particular gait. Do we not all walk, jog and run? When we stand still, are our feet not turned out slightly? When we jog, do they not straighten up? Is it not obvious that for different situations or speeds our body automatically adopts a more suitable, natural posture? It seems that it is not so obvious. In fighting should we not both wrestle and box, and become accustomed to both light and heavy weapons and the differences inherent within? Kendo practitioners always point their feet forwards, even though they do not move. Karate practitioners commonly practise in a sideways stance, both feet pointing to the right, or both to the left. Shodokan Aikido practitioners always keep the forward foot straight. Yoshinkan practitioners always turn the front foot out. Perhaps we should ask ourselves what happened to nature. Did a horse ever have the idea to change the natural positions of its feet? No, but man has the stupidity to teach the horse new gaits for the sake of fashion. Musashi, infamous master of the Japanese duel, took 'no-stance' as his stance, and gave it no name, claiming that it was no different from the way he walked along the path.

In Aikido, the general rule is to move and turn on the balls of the feet, although many a master will occasionally be observed using the heels. Obviously, the way we use our feet should be affected more by practical realities than by set rules.

Shizen-hontai

Shizen-hontai means 'natural posture' and is a term more commonly associated with Judo than Aikido. Typically, it refers to a feet-turned-slightly-outwards, shoulder-width-apart, legs-ever-so-slightly-bent neutral standing position; *aikidoka* see it as a more advanced type of posture of no-posture whereas in Judo it is considered quite basic. Practising from a left or right posture for several years, an *aikidoka* might find it somewhat awkward at first, but will soon come to love it.

5 Breathing

Just do it. *Nike advertising slogan*

Everyone breathes. Athletes of any sport co-ordinate their breathing with their movement without thinking about it. Of course, they will only really think about it if they become professional, and by that time, they will probably have got it right. In Aikido, we are forced to learn breathing from the beginning before even knowing the forms. No wonder it appears so mysterious.

Exercises

Exercises prepare the body for training in two ways. First, the body is warmed up by gentle then harder exercise and stretching. During this time it is important to mobilize the major muscle groups and to stretch in all directions. There is no need for excessive strength conditioning in an *aiki* warm-up, indeed, it would have the effect of killing your *aiki*, not nourishing it. Second, during the various exercises it is important to breathe in rhythm. If you move fast, you should breathe fast; if you move slowly, you should breathe slowly. This is natural.

When sitting at the beginning of class, you should become aware of your slow breathing. If it is not already slow, make it so, by taking deliberate, slow breaths to slow down the heartbeat. When sitting after vigorous practice, your breathing rate will be rapid but you should maintain control of it. Breathing too fast demonstrates a lack of conscious control, but consciously breathing too slowly at this time might cause you to feel faint. Instead, you should concentrate on breathing deeply, and the air should enter as though filling a large jug – from the bottom. This will allow you to calm down both physically and mentally.

Constant attention to the breathing during warm-up exercises and stretching routines will help you to establish an unconscious link between breathing and movement that will eventually carry over into your techniques, and into your everyday life.

Kokyu-ho

Kokyu-ho translates as 'breathing exercise'. Basically, the *kokyu-ho* movements are designed to help co-ordinate *aiki* movement with breathing. The emphasis here is on the co-ordination of movement with breathing, not on the technique or throw. This is simply because, once you have a technique as your objective, everything else is often forgotten. By having no technique, you can concentrate on the essential task at hand – co-ordination.

What is often forgotten is that *uke* is also learning how to co-ordinate his own breathing with his own movement at the same time. One golden rule is for neither *tori* nor *uke* to strain excessively or hold the breath. To develop *kokyu* it is necessary to practise against ever-stronger grips; you need to build a strong base for the flowing techniques that come later. *Kokyu-ho* exercises are ideal for gaining insight into understanding *aiki*.

Kokyu-nage

Kokyu-nage translates as 'breath throw'. As an extension of *kokyu-ho*, *kokyu-nage* results in a throw. Although it can sometimes seem complicated, the throw is usually not much more than a simple step and push. Obviously, keeping it simple aids the learning process. Here, you are learning to co-ordinate your body movement with the breath while throwing down, or projecting away. As in *kokyu-ho*, at no point should *tori* or *uke* excessively strain or hold the breath; both should breathe out during the movement. In fact, on hitting the ground gently, *uke*'s breath is gentle; if hitting hard, the breath naturally exhales more sharply, but still without strain or restriction.

Kokyu-ho and *kokyu-nage* collectively attempt to develop a feeling of solid *aiki* and bridge the gap between basic and advanced technique, thereby producing good Aikido. With *kokyu-nage*, the body becomes accustomed to the larger movements and principles; with less technical detail, the student can learn more efficiently.

One important point to note here is that *kokyu-nage* is not a technique. If *kokyu-nage* is regarded as just another technique on a grading syllabus then its essence cannot be ascertained or acquired. Accordingly, it is wise not to name the various forms of *kokyu-nage* that exist lest they become rigid techniques. Another important point is that more allowance for variation in *kokyu-nage* should be tolerated, allowing *tori* the freedom to experiment to figure it out. It goes without saying that *kokyu-nage* techniques are useful in

learning how to deal with powerful grips in such a way that you can move or throw *uke* efficiently. In fact, as your skill at *kokyu-nage* develops, you begin to merge with *uke*'s movement and *aiki* can develop. Eventually, *tori* will learn to become more in tune with *uke* and the skills acquired, a certain *aiki* feeling, will transfer over into the standard techniques and set the student off along a new voyage of discovery.

Kiai

Kiai, which means literally 'energy in harmony', but translates more realistically as 'focused energy', refers to the shout that is sometimes emitted during the execution of a technique. Some schools teach it with every technique, some only when using weapons, while others never do it. As is usual, the middle way provides the best route. Of course, the *kiai* originates from the breath exhaling from the lungs but a measure of power can be added by contracting the stomach muscles to help push the breath out. The result is a feeling that the sound is actually emanating from the pit of the stomach. Accordingly, the sound is deep and powerful. Students should be careful in trying to produce this; one common mistake is simply to growl or scowl loudly from the throat.

Schools of Aikido generally use the *Ei* sound to *kiai*. Other sounds commonly heard are *Ai, Ka, To, Suh, Sa, Hai, Ho*, and so on. Some schools even credit certain sounds with purpose. For example, one might be offensive and another defensive. However, as there is no apparent uniformity of usage between schools, it is difficult to establish whether such distinctions can be based on true nature.

For *tori*, depending upon the school, the *kiai* is emitted at the beginning or the end of the technique and signifies a counterstrike, the break of a joint, or even the kill.

26

For *uke*, the *kiai* is either emitted at the beginning when attacking, or, less commonly, as an aid to the break-fall at the end, to signify 'hitting' the ground in a more 'positive' manner.

One problem with the *kiai* is that it demands one hundred per cent of the body's energy in the moment, and if the student's technique is ineffective, it will be wasted energy, leaving him vulnerable to counter-attack. Therefore, many prefer not to *kiai* in ordinary *aiki* training, and use it only in more solitary training or weapons practice. It is also possible for the *kiai* to be silent, as a strongly focused breath, the shorter the sharper. A common example of this is the sharp outward breath made during a hard break-fall to protect the body, especially if *tori* falls on top of *uke*, as often happens in Judo.

Meditation

Many people in martial arts can be seen sitting apparently in meditation, but understanding the 'how' of it is not so easy. In Japanese, meditation is *mokuso*, which translates literally as 'silent thought'. The *dojo* is often likened to a temple where the martial artist can go to escape the trivialities of ordinary life, so this is where we sit quietly to forget, actively seeking that which we can only passively attain, the ever-elusive *satori*, or enlightenment.

We leave the outside world behind us when we enter the *dojo*. By forgetting, we empty our minds for a new experience. In the temple, that new experience involves 'sitting' and tuning yourself to nature. In this busy world, people are often frustrated when they have nothing to do. Others are frustrated when they have too much to do. For the monk, meditation is the solution. In the *dojo*, there is more. Sitting at rest is concentrated relaxation, the gathering of energy. This is not merely sitting and relaxing; rather, you will be filling your body with *aiki* of the unbendable arm nature.

In addition, both *tori* and *uke* must strive to maintain their *aiki* meditative state while in motion – this leads to the idea of Aikido as 'Moving Zen'.

After practice, the breathing rate may be increased. At this time, the student sits and concentrates on maintaining control of the breath. Of course, it follows that if you can maintain control of the breath while practising Aikido, you will rarely be out of breath, nor need consciously to control it either during or after practice. If you are out of breath after vigorous practice then sitting quietly allows further insight into meditation. As your chest spontaneously moves up and down in the body's quest for oxygen, you take conscious control. The emphasis here is on learning to take control. In time, you will also learn to take control when sitting quietly at the beginning of the class, even though you are not tired. In martial arts there is a before, during and after aspect to breathing.

Some teachers incorporate breathing deeply and slowly with meditation; some include quiet music or other rhythm. The usual emphasis is on the deeper and the slower, which is good practice. However, you should be aware of – or be wary of – the fact that the teacher's rhythm may not be the same as your own. While it is polite discipline to follow the teacher's rhythm, ultimately the student must find and follow his own rhythm.

It is also important to keep in mind that the purpose of meditative breathing is to improve your martial ability.

Breathing Rhythm

Students often ask whether they should breathe in or out at a particular time. In martial arts the moment of inhalation is considered as being inherently weak, offering an opening for attack. Therefore, the only answer can be to breathe in quickly, and out slowly. If this still does not satisfy the curious mind, the guideline is that it is best to breathe out when doing the work. If you are tired, getting up off the floor can be considered to be work, so breathe out as you get up, but inhale before *uke* attacks. If you are not tired, you can inhale while rising, hold the breath slightly, not straining at all, and then exhale as *uke* attacks and you perform the technique. *Uke* should also exhale when attacking, and continue to breathe as *tori* performs the technique.

The reason why you should avoid straining the breath, keeping the trachea open, is that you will be more relaxed if you are caught unawares. Indeed, with no real weight to deal with in Aikido, there is less need to strain. The heavier the weight, as in weight-lifting, the more the breath will strain, but this is a natural strain that develops power. Weight-lifters never actually stop breathing, and it is through breathing that they get a more total co-ordination of power.

There is a natural rhythm to breathing in many sports and that rhythm is always related to movement. A swimmer's head turns out of the water and takes a breath on a predetermined number of strokes according to speed and fitness. Likewise, a runner breathes a predetermined number of breaths according to the number of steps taken. For example, a 2-2 breathing system means he breathes in for two steps and out for two steps. Of course it follows that there is also a 2-1 system, a 3-3 system, a 2-3 system, a 3-2 system, and so on. If he tires, he slows and switches from, say, a 2-2 system to a 3-3. When sprinting to the finish line, he uses a 2-1 system. (In running, stride length is also important. It might seem obvious but, if after running along a flat road you suddenly run up a hill, your body will automatically 'change down a gear' and the stride will shorten, while maintaining frequency. We like to keep the rhythm.)

When cutting with the sword in Aikido you could make one, two, three or four steps per cut, depending on how fast you move, and it follows that your breathing could be one breath out per cut, or perhaps, one breath out per two cuts. Few will teach this so it remains for discerning students to figure out variations for themselves.

6 The Mind

The appearance of an 'enemy' should be thought of as an opportunity to test the sincerity of one's mental and physical training. *O Sensei*

The mind is a very complicated thing to comprehend. It controls us while we try to think about it. How can we gain a measure of conscious control over the mind?

Co-Ordination

In Aikido, we practise everything equally on the left and right sides. While this can be very confusing in the beginning, it leads to improved co-ordination of mind and body alike, as a literal translation of the word 'Aikido' implies, and allows us to see more clearly what others are doing. It increases dexterity, and balances out unevenness in the mind and body. Some schools emphasize one side only; in terms of the reality of self-defence, this can be a practical method, but the inquisitive student should require more than that.

Focus

Concentration is the most mysterious of powers. Who could measure it? Can its existence be proven? Who could produce it outside of the body? In a sense, it does not exist yet no one would deny it can be of tremendous power. Some people have it all, others have none. What is important is that it can be developed, and it must be, otherwise you will never be able to learn Aikido. Concentration is necessary to learn any new skill and once you have developed it, it remains available for use elsewhere, in education or in business.

Determination is as mysterious as concentration and is necessary for success in overcoming obstacles. Too much may blind you to the reality of your misdirection and too little will go far in achieving nothing. Concentration and determination are apparent in the frowning gaze and alert tension of the body and result in the student being in focus for the moment.

Visible concentration and focus.

Zanshin

Zanshin, which translates as 'remaining mind' or is sometimes called 'concentrated concentration', is commonly referred to as that state of mind that is kept when finishing a technique. For example, in table tennis a good player plans his shot a moment ahead in time and imagines it striking home; the spectator may see him focusing on the ball for a moment even after it has gone past his opponent, just making sure, and focusing on that moment. A broader interpretation of *zanshin* can be likened to being behind the wheel of a car, for which the driver needs constant awareness. In Aikido, we need to develop these three kinds of *zanshin*: before, during and after.

Usually, awareness is aroused at the beginning of class with the initial bow. Here, concentration increases. During practice, *tori*'s awareness will increase when bowing to *uke*. It will increase further as *uke* prepares to attack. At this moment, the concentration becomes determination. After much practice, the martial artist's awareness should be apparent all the time, sometimes broad, sometimes focused. Awareness can also be divided according

Maintaining focus after the technique is finished.

30

to the *yin/yang* principle. A *yang* type of awareness might be overt whereas a *yin* type might remain somewhat hidden, yet present. In martial terms, awareness is a changing mix of alert concentration and alert determination, which in combination signify that you are wide awake.

Calm Mind

The natural adrenalin-based instinct of fight or flight is a response that might result in more trouble than you bargained for. You have to overcome it, as only then can it be utilized to advantage. The calm mind is a controlled mind. Anger in the mind will be detrimental to the workings of the body, both in terms of health and of technique. A calm mind allows you to have a broader view, in which things fall into their natural perspective. A calm mind can sum up a rapidly deteriorating situation in a short space of time. That same calm mind is likely to offer a clearer solution. And if a decision is made to act, the adrenalin may still be there, if it is needed.

The Inner Eye

The inner eye, or mind's eye, is the eye through which you see your self. It is particularly useful, for example, when learning new techniques. In the beginning, the student may become confused with all the movement being demonstrated, not knowing where to place his gaze. Should I watch the hands? Should I watch the feet? Worse, he may fall into the trap of just watching the spectacle of the demonstration after which he will not have the slightest clue of where to start. With the mind's eye, you can place your self in the teacher's shoes, and, while sitting and watching, you can imagine going through the same technique as the teacher in real time.

Another use of the mind's eye is to visualize something before it happens, and therefore respond 'in time' accordingly. Good soccer players often visualize the ball going into the net the moment just before they shoot. In Aikido, using the mind's eye, the practitioner can learn to anticipate *uke*'s attack and thus can move slightly before *uke* arrives, and take the lead.

With beginners, if *uke* attacks before *tori* is ready, then *tori* will be taken by surprise and will not react until the mind clears and good measure is taken of the situation. This is no good. To solve this, before offering the hand to be grabbed, *tori* should quickly imagine what needs to be done. If *uke* rushes forwards too soon, tell him 'No!' Going through it once, in the mind, leads to a better result. Once ready, *tori* offers the hand, *uke* grasps, and the technique is performed like clockwork. Perhaps not the spontaneous *aiki* of your dreams, but a beginning. The more you practise, the shorter the thinking time becomes. It is a practical route to 'no-thought' for those who do not want to waste a lifetime hoping that one day 'it'll just happen'.

Gaze

Some recommend that you should watch the eyes for intention. Depending upon intensity, looking into the eyes can instil aggressiveness, firmness, confidence or calmness. Looking away might convey nonchalance, doubt, insecurity or fear. The true spirit can be hidden and all can be used to advantage. Others say you should watch the body or shoulders for clues of movement; the hips or shoulders move a certain way before a punch. Perhaps watching the body really means that you are avoiding the eyes. The school of thought that avoids the eyes advises variously that you should watch the point between the eyes, watch the chest, watch a point beyond the attacker, and so on.

Table tennis is a very fast game and common advice is to watch the ball. However, while the table tennis player needs to know where the ball is, there is no need to look at it. With experience, he instinctively knows where to find it. In fact, when playing, the player has to see everything. In the ultimate shot in table tennis, the player gauges his opponent's intention so well that he can lead him about at will and then, with a slow nonchalant flick, send the ball to one corner just as he rushes in lured anticipation to the other. In table tennis doubles, the skill lies in being able to make the opponents collide into each other. This is not done by watching the ball. Another analogy is driving a car. If the driver only looks at and follows the car in front, road signs will be missed and a crash may result. He needs to look at nothing in particular, yet see everything.

Aikido is the same. When training, even in the midst of technique, students should take the time to gaze around, see who is where, listen, hear, take note of what else is going on in the *dojo*, see safe space – no one is there, no one is coming, throw *uke* down. *Uke* needs to be aware, too. Accidents in the *dojo* happen when people are not aware of what is going on around them, and training in a crowded *dojo* can be good practice. In time, knowing where to throw and where you are being thrown will become automatic.

7 Space

Ma-ai is the distance at which combatants engage each other; as this distance is shortened, the courage and skill of the warrior must be increased. *Donn F. Draeger*

You should always be aware of your surroundings with a view to self-protection and even the *dojo* is designed with protection in mind. The entrance is ideally to the rear left corner (when facing the front, or *kamiza*), where the lowest students traditionally sit. The teacher sits at the front with his back to the wall, keeping the door in full view. If the teacher wanders near the door, he should become a little more aware of that potential source of danger, not turning his back on it. If a madman suddenly enters, those of more ability at the further end of the *dojo* will have more time to react. The *dojo* is the teacher's space and it is designed for them alone. The next time you are in a public place, choose where to sit a little more carefully.

Distance

Distance, or *ma-ai*, refers to the starting position in Aikido from where *uke* usually initiates a one-step attack against *tori* and this distance is usually determined by your

Negotiating distance.

Ready to attack.

reach. For standing techniques, *tori* and *uke* will be at least one *tatami* length apart, but less than two, and this should be slightly different for every partner. For kneeling techniques, or *suwari-waza*, as the step is shorter, so is the initial starting distance. Typically, the distance is within one *tatami* length.

In preparation for the attack the ideal *uke* gets the distance correct; *tori* just waits. Sometimes, *tori* and *uke* can be seen continually shuffling about in preparation. This scenario occurs when each is sure that their interpretation of distance is correct, and that the other is at fault. Clearly, something needs to be sorted out, but it could also be a reflection of *tori* and *uke* being of a different size. Certain schools maintain different distances; some start closer, others further apart. This cannot be right, as distance cannot be set exactly.

It goes without saying that putting a weapon in your hand increases the distance by at least the length of that weapon. When both partners hold swords, *uke* should typically be a 'one-step-attack' away from *tori* in terms of either *tsugi-ashi* or *ayumi-ashi*. When standing, the swords do not cross. If the swords cross, the fight has already started. Instead, the minimum distance between the two extended swords should be at least a few inches. It could be much more, being determined by how far you could leap to strike, or, at the extreme, even the distance you could accurately throw a dagger, or fear it to be thrown.

Unfortunately, in modern Japanese arts, very little thought is given to correct distance or length of weapons. Assuming the weapons to be of the same length, which they almost always are, the remaining variables are length of arm, length of stride and length of lunge. Since these are clearly different for every practitioner, this means there can be no set distance; its measurement can only be 'negotiated' in the moment by each of the pair as they face each other. One with a longer arm, stride and lunge would feel 'ready' and capable of attack at a relatively long range, while the partner might want to edge a little closer, although he might do so rather warily. Naturally, opponents' tactics might differ too. For example, someone who is taller and longer in stride and reach might be more aggressive, while a shorter person might be more defensive.

If both are free to choose a weapon, it might be that a short, stocky swordsman with shorter arms would prefer to hold a longer, but heavier sword closer to his centre, whereas a tall, lanky, small-framed swordsman might decide upon a shorter, lighter one. If that shorter swordsman decides to thrust suddenly, holding with just one hand at the bottom end of the handle, he will gain several inches in an instant. Of course, all things being equal, if the object is to stick the sharp point into an opponent, the tall person with the longer reach holds the advantage. But things are never all equal, nor does the best fighter always win.

When holding a *jo* (staff), much of the above holds true. When partners face each other, the staves should not cross. Each partner should only be concerned about his own correct distance. Some shuffling is normal. If the opponent is too close, then you may either thrust if you feel confident, or retreat if you feel unsure. Again, as in sword work, *uke* typically starts from a distance of 'one-step-attack' away. However, as the staff is longer than the sword, so the initial distance should be greater. In addition, *tori* should be at a distance whereby it is possible to step back just one step to avoid a long-range one handed round-house-type strike, typically to the knee.

For each unequal pair there will be one optimal 'negotiated' distance. Both *tori* and *uke* have to figure out this optimal distance as a pair. In so doing, they will both learn how to fit together harmoniously, and, later, they will also learn that they can take advantage of mistakes their partners make in their measurement of distance.

When using the *tanto* in Aikido, typically one person has it, the other does not. It should be immediately obvious that the one who has it has the advantage of distance. Starting in a posture with hand and *tanto* crossed is ridiculous, and this should establish the principle that starting in this way when both *tori* and *uke* have empty hands is also wrong. For a principle to be a principle it should stand the test of logic and carry over into other situations. Typically, the attack starts from one step away, and *uke* may decide to add spice and 'poke' *tori* should a *suki* (gap) emerge in their technique.

Aikidoka do not normally kick. However, they should be in such a position that it would be possible to do so, should they wish. Thinking like this will help the student to learn the correct distance to maintain during the technique. Careful consideration here will show that certain set distances can be established. This means that the feet should be close enough to deliver a low side kick, a low instep kick, a knee to the ribs as *uke* comes down (as in *ikkyo*), a step on the foot, or a trip. If any of the latter are possible, it is fair to say that the distance is good, but if between distances, and such counter-attack is not possible, then the distance could be said to be compromised.

The attack gives *tori* something to work with, hence the phrase 'no attack, no technique'. In *Budo*, martial training, the best

Sword is shorter than optimal length.

time to act is early and, therefore, it is useful for *tori* to train to close the distance.

Weapon Length

The most distinctive feature of weapons in Japanese martial arts is that they are almost all of the same length. In *Paradoxes of Defence* (1599), George Silver calculates the correct length of a one-handed sword to be, with the sword arm's (right) elbow fully drawn back, long enough to uncross the swordsman's own dagger, or, in other words, to reach the fingers in the outstretched opposite (left) hand. Any longer, it advises, would result in the swordsman being unable to disengage rapidly if crossed (by withdrawing the elbow). Any shorter, it advises, would result in the swordsman not taking advantage of his physical size.

In the past, the size of the English short staff (up to 9ft long) was calculated according to height and arm length. Staff-fighting was divided into short- and long-range versions. Short-range fighting called for a half-staff position, in which the practitioner held the staff a quarter-length from each end, thereby holding half the length between the hands. In long-range quarter-staff fighting, the fighter held the lower quarter-length end of the staff with the point squared at the opponent. Thus, there were two completely different strategies combined for one weapon.

While there may be different methods of calculating the correct length of a weapon, what is readily apparent in Aikido is that they are all the same. No thought is given to the physical size of the martial artists, although on rare occasions some do speak of a ground-to-armpit length measure for the *jo*. If you happen to see an old Japanese suit of armour in a museum with a *katana* next to it, you will not fail to notice how small that suit is in relation to the length of the accompanying sword. Surely, for a long-armed six-foot Anglo-Saxon a modern standard Japanese *katana* must be rather short. The blade of my own *bokken* is 29.5in; according to Silver's method, my six-foot frame could handle a blade 9.5in longer.

Some say that the movement of the *jo* in Aikido represents that of a spear, but it must be a very short spear. Perhaps someone chopped the pointed part off an old spear for training purposes and then forgot to add a bit of extra length to make up for it. Spears are long, usually much longer than staves. Another possibility is that O Sensei incorporated Jukendo (bayonet) movements into his Aikido training using the *jo*; he was known for his prowess at Jukendo whilst training the Japanese military. Further evidence that the *jo* is not a staff can be found in the fact that in Jodo, the Japanese art of the short staff, the techniques are quite different, being more suited to a weapon the size of the *jo*. If Japanese weapons appear to prefer tradition over common sense, it should also be pointed out that, after the invention of the gun in Renaissance Europe, the design of swords was more likely to be dictated by gentlemen's fashion than by function.

What is most important in Aikido practice is to search for and maintain common principles in terms of co-ordination, space and time. The lessons learned with the *bokken* ought to correspond and not conflict with what is learned with the *jo* or empty hand. Weapons training offers insight into common principles and, if it is ignored, the student is likely to end up practising separate arts, and, though he may spend a lifetime at his task, he might never understand. No one is likely to become a sword master by studying Aikido. If that is your aim, you must study Kenjutsu. Simply put, the purpose of weapons practice in Aikido is to provide foundation for the empty-hand techniques.

8 Time

We must use time as a tool, not as a crutch.
John F. Kennedy

The *irimi* and *tenkan*, or, as some say, *omote* and *ura* versions of techniques can be thought of as being suitable for different situations. For example, if *uke* pulls, *tori* could enter and perform an *irimi*-type of technique. If *uke* pushes, then *tori* could perform a *tenkan*-type of technique. Another way of looking at the difference is in terms of how *tori* leads *uke*'s energy. In performing an *irimi* variant, *tori* is effectively returning *uke*'s energy back towards *uke* and beyond. When performing *tenkan*, *tori* adds a little to *uke*'s energy, initially encouraging it on, outwards, in the direction it was going, then redirecting it.

A third way of rationalizing *irimi* and *tenkan* is in terms of time. Training with time in mind adds an air of reality to practice, yet training in timing is rarely specifically targeted in Aikido or other Japanese martial arts. Timing exists, of course, and it is learned unconsciously. Without a framework, however, many people do not actually know what it is that they know. Nor can they easily teach it. Some timing-related concepts and exercises are described below.

Provoking the Attack
Tori feints towards *uke*, who responds by raising his own arm in defence. *Tori* then takes *uke*'s raised arm and performs a technique. The initial feint is *irimi* in nature, but only if the body moves forward, as in an *irimi*-type technique (if the arm only moves, it cannot be called *irimi*; it is just a feint in Aikido). At this time, especially if *uke* stumbles back slightly, then *tori* can take initiative with an *irimi* movement. However, if *uke* responds a little more strongly preventing an *irimi* entry, then *tori* performs a *tenkan* movement.

A typical example of this timing is *shomen-uchi ikkyo irimi*, where *tori* initiates the attack and takes control as *uke* raises his arm in defence.

Before the Attack
It takes *uke* a short moment to invigorate and prepare his energy for attack. *Tori* attacks before he is fully ready.

As *uke* Prepares for the Attack (i)
As *uke* raises his arm in preparation for *shomen-uchi*, *tori* rushes in harmonizing with the upward movement, then performs a technique. If *tori*'s entry is quick and in harmony, the result will be an *irimi* technique.

As *uke* Prepares for the Attack (ii)
Tori rushes in just as *uke* has begun a *shomen-uchi* attack. It is almost a clash, but if *tori* catches it early enough, *uke* will be overcome by a combination of *tori*'s forward momentum and the element of surprise, and an *irimi* technique is likely to result.

Tori meets the attack early.

During the Attack

As *uke* begins to strike down with *shomen-uchi*, *tori* moves forwards quickly to meet it in the same time, and, on meeting, turns and deflects it slightly, adding energy to it. *Tori* typically moves ever so slightly to the side to avoid meeting the attack head on. Meeting at this slightly later point in time, uke's energy usually requires *tori* to perform a *tenkan* technique. However, while the initial movement is *tenkan* in nature,

tori might decide to follow up with an *irimi* technique. While practising, *tori* can have the feeling of starting late, catching up and overtaking, or moving at the same time in direct co-ordination and total harmony with *uke*.

Total Harmony

Total harmony with the attack occurs when *tori* harmonizes with *uke*'s movement in both of the latter two phases. As

Tori meets the attack midway.

uke raises for *shomen-uchi*, *tori* does like-wise; as *uke* cuts, *tori* cuts too and makes technique by adding energy and redirect-ing. Here, *tori* harmonizes with *uke*'s preparation and attack, a good starting point to master before altering the time. Strangely, the more you practise in har-mony, the easier it becomes to change the time.

Disturbing the Attack

As *uke* cuts down with *shomen-uchi*, *tori* cuts up, hitting *uke*'s strike at a tangent, contacting on or near the elbow and deflecting it slightly off course. *Tori* follows through with a new cut, adding energy to *uke*'s arm. If the follow-up cut is fast, a *tenkan* technique will result; if it is slow and *uke* recovers slightly, *irimi* is natural.

As *uke* cuts down, *tori* raises his arm up to deflect.

The feeling in the deflection is as if trying to knock something out of *uke*'s hand mid-swing.

After the Attack (i)

That point in time after a powerful *shomen-uchi* or *tsuki* lunge in which *uke* has momentarily over-extended himself is another opportunity waiting to be taken. At this exact moment, *uke* may be wide open for an incapacitating strike and adding a little energy to *uke*'s direction of imbalance offers an opening to begin a *tenkan* technique.

After the Attack (ii)

After *uke* has over-extended it is natural to recover. In this instance, *tori* should immediately harmonize with *uke*'s retreat and move in for an *irimi* technique.

41

Uke's attack has momentarily expired.

It is apparent, then, that the distinction between when you should and should not perform an *irimi*- or *tenkan*-type technique can be based upon the time of meeting *uke*'s energy. It should also be pointed out that it is possible to mix *irimi* and *tenkan* together. You can start with an *irimi* movement and finish with *tenkan*, and vice versa, but this is not recommended in gradings, when you are supposed to keep them separate in order to show that you do indeed recognize the distinctions. Of course, those keen to learn Aikido should be aware that the above distinctions are rarely, if ever, taught in any rational framework.

Fencing Time

All martial arts deal with timing but few appear to provide a clear structural framework of principles that embody timing as a principle in itself. Italian schools of fencing combine time with method to produce strategy. With a little imagination it ought not be too difficult to transfer their concepts of timing to any martial art. It would be even better to structure your own training to incorporate it formally.

In fencing, for example, one aggressive or one defensive movement is labelled as being done in one time, irrespective of the speed of the movement. The different principles of time are as follows:

- *duo tempo* (double time) is the simplest to understand and practise, but the easiest to defend against. Here, block/parry and counter-strike make two completely separate movements;
- *mezzo tempo* (middle time) involves countering the attack as it develops, sometimes with the feeling of overtaking it;
- *in tempo* (in time, or stop hit) avoids and counter-strikes in harmony with the attack, in the same time;
- *stesso tempo* (one time) means intercepting, deflecting the attack, and countering all in the same time;
- *contra tempo* (counter time) means that a counter-attack is provoked, and exploited.

Writing about swordplay, George Silver in his *Paradoxes of Defence* (London, 1599) identifies his *four true times*:

1. time of the hand;
2. time of the hand and body;
3. time of the hand, body and foot; and
4. time of the hand, body and feet.

His *four false times* are also identified:

1. time of the foot;
2. time of the foot and body;
3. time of the foot, body and hand; and
4. time of the feet, body and hand.

Interestingly, Aikido, a body art whose motion originates in the centre, appears to be based on Silver's *false* times.

Techniques without time are nothing more than dead form. Training in the tempo of movement is a priceless tool of strategy; the martial artist can anticipate and predict or lure to create the immediate future. However, it must be remembered that European fencing is a hand art whereas Aikido is primarily a body art. As such, Aikido offers a few more variations, such as taking the balance, adding energy to the attack, and looking for openings in the midst of movement to a different range of target techniques.

One thing to be wary of is that many basic Aikido techniques are based on the simplest and most basic Italian concept, *duo tempo*. If you have the knowledge of where you are in time, you can modify it to be different. It is a sensible learning strategy to isolate examples of various times within Aikido training and to memorize and practise them.

9 From Avoidance to Contact

There is no avoiding war, it can only be postponed to the advantage of others. *Niccoló dei Machiavelli*

Best not to be there. Best not to let the situation deteriorate. And if you are there, it is best to lose a bit of pride than to come to heated argument or violent exchange of blows. However, you cannot, and should not, avoid every unsavoury situation. At times, you just have to argue your point to illuminate ignorance, or fight for what you know to be right. And when the fight is right, avoidance manifests itself in physical movement.

Evasion

To avoid an attack, you need to practise moving in eight directions: forward and back, right and left, two corners to the front, and two to the rear. Many schools have a methodological routine for practising this, many do not, but it is necessary to practise both alone and with a partner. It is also possible to avoid in an up and down direction, and by turning. Of course, the student should practise turning, or *tais-abaki*, along the eight directions too, both clockwise and anti-clockwise. The golden rule is not to look at the hands or feet while moving. Instead, look at nothing in particular, yet see everything.

An excellent, perhaps indispensable, method of practising avoidance is training with the *bokken* and the *jo*. Training with these tools teaches the student to move out of the way of his partner's attack simply because it is so painful not to. However, it is important to take great care that the postures and movements made when using weapons are the same as those when performing Aikido, otherwise, you will be learning separate arts; unfortunately, this is all too common.

As Aikido is a body art, it follows that any movement in avoidance should originate from the body's centre. One way to get a feeling for this is to clasp the hands behind the back, stretching out the chest and belly somewhat. Have *uke* punch fast, but not hard, and avoid it just enough so that it barely touches the chest or belly. It should feel as though *uke*'s thrusting arm turns your own body.

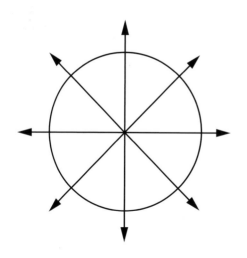

Eight directions.

Move to the right and parry.

Move to the left and parry.

Ninin-dori or *tanin-dori* training can be used to develop avoidance skills. *Uke*s simply rush *tori*, who moves out of the way and pushes them away. After a while, the push can be converted to *kokyu-nage*. This sort of practice is often seen in demonstrations where *tori* seemingly throws six or seven *uke*s repeatedly, often with the keen spectator casting a critical eye. This method is excellent for developing avoidance and co-ordination skills but it does not represent real skill in dealing with multiple attackers. Accordingly, this method of practice should be confined to the *dojo*. It is a means, not the end.

Different Approaches in Principle

If you are pushed at the shoulder from the front, you can take the following actions.

45

1. Just move out of the way to the side and avoid the push.
2. Step back with one or two steps rigidly, with no give in the body. *Tori* moves because *uke* shoves. Posture is maintained and the feeling is a little wooden. Training in this way may develop a correspondingly rigid attitude in the mind. There are benefits to this approach for some.
3. Step back with one or two steps, with give, rather floppy in the upper body, to the left or right depending upon which side was pushed. *Tori*'s posture may be lost slightly if the push is strong, hence the rearward step. *Uke* may overbalance and *tori* can use this to begin technique. However, if *tori* himself becomes off-balance with this passive method the chance may be lost.
4. Step back quickly, in time with the push; the body feels floppy to *uke* but it is not. *Tori* retreats in harmony with *uke*'s push. *Uke* feels as though his push peters out to nothing. *Tori* is in full control; *uke* may have lost balance.
5. Step back in time with the push, but, more than stepping back, say, with the left, the feeling is of turning, and pressing the right side forwards, decisively, with intent. Here, *tori* is already upon *uke* and the emphasis is on forward counter-attack.

It cannot be said that one measure is better than another – all exist, all are possible, and all should be given consideration. Indeed, a person of weak disposition might benefit from training in the second method, as this may toughen them up mentally somewhat. Allowing an aggressor to shove you will demonstrate clearly to all those present who is initiating the trouble. Furthermore, receiving a couple of hard shoves might even satisfy the antagonist, thereby dissolving the situation.

Contact

Avoidance does not mean 'no-contact'. As *tori* retreats, *uke* can be lured or pulled, as *tori* turns, *uke* can be pushed. Sometimes there is no direct physical contact; *tori* avoids while carefully maintaining a certain physical distance, anything from a few millimetres to a few centimetres. Here, *tori* moves in decisive harmony with *uke* just as sure as if they were actually in direct contact. When *tori* retreats it can be somewhat like the feeling of the reverse poles of two magnets pressing each other without touching, after which time *tori* then reverses polarity, following and adding to *uke*'s energy to effect technique. A sensible place to start in the search for correct contact is with grips.

'Contact' means that feeling of meeting *uke*, gently, yet firmly. The feeling should also be the same when *uke* meets *tori*. Different schools grip with different strengths but within each school it tends to be uniform. Some schools grip very lightly, some grip firmly, and others grip like a vice. The first thing that is apparent to the observer is that those schools that grip lightly rarely grip strongly, and criticize those that do. Similarly, those that grip strongly seldom grip lightly, and criticize those that do. Clearly, something is amiss.

Common sense would recommend that all methods be used with a compromise settling on being *firm*, or 'taking up the slack'. When *uke* grabs *tori*'s wrist, *uke* pushes forwards slightly from the centre, taking up the slack in the skin that exists between the two hands. Once the slack is taken up, the grip is said to be 'firm'. Likewise, *tori* can also take up the slack by pushing forwards slightly from the centre, but he should not need to since it is *uke*'s job to attack.

Some describe 'firm' as meaning 'no gap'. This means that *uke* should try to hold on and not let any gap appear between his hand and *tori*'s wrist; *uke* should maintain contact throughout *tori*'s technique, which is, in essence, interpreted as maintaining the attack. However, this does not mean that he should contort himself to *tori*'s bad technique. There are two aspects here that need consideration. First, *tori* should be aware that the more comfortable *uke* feels, the better they are controlling and dealing with him. This does not mean 'no-pain', rather, it means that *tori* should give *uke* comfortable space to occupy, and an easy means to fall, or receive technique. Second, if *tori* does make *uke* feel uncomfortable, then it is done by rational choice, not badly controlled technique.

Both of these concepts – 'taking up the slack' and 'no gap' – are easy to come to terms with. At the moment of touching, both *tori* and *uke* should rotate their hips forwards and up. This ensures connection and stability between the upper and lower halves of the body, and helps each 'feel' the other's centre. If *uke*'s hips are not extended forwards and up, then it feels like a lacklustre attack – and it will look that way to an observer, too. Worse still, *uke* gives the impression of being in fear.

Once this idea of establishing correct contact is understood, *tori* and *uke* can practise very lightly, or very strongly, yet still perform responsive Aikido that is conducive to developing *aiki*. Therefore, it is not a question of whether the training is hard or soft, the key is maintaining correct contact.

At the moment of contact, the centre of body weight should be mostly, or all, over

Keeping the foot, knee and shoulder in line is important in positioning the hips to develop contact.

the front leg/foot to facilitate turning (*tenkan*). The closer the centre is to the point of contact, the more efficient the turn. Indeed, the best position for *tori*'s centre is right over or under the targeted point of contact on *uke*. Contact can also be considered as a form of strike and this goes some way towards explaining how Aikido is sometimes interpreted as being 90 per cent *atemi*.

10 Balance

I don't know what effect these men will have upon the enemy, but, by God, they terrify me. *Duke of Wellington*

Taking another's balance is easier said than done, but if done well, the throw becomes a foregone conclusion. *Uke* can be tricked, lured, tripped, distracted, struck, pushed or pulled off balance.

From Eight to Two Directions

Teachers often speak of *happo*, or 'eight directions'. What it means is that *tori* can evade in eight directions, off-balance *uke* in eight directions, and counter-attack in eight directions. It is a useful schemata for solo exercises, but it is not easy to think of eight directions while training with a rapidly moving partner; in this case, it is far easier to limit it to two – the body bending forwards and backwards, sometimes forwards and a little to the left, sometimes backwards and a little to the right. *Tori* just concentrates on the forwards/backwards distinction, any variation being the result of where *uke* pulls, pushes, or just plain falls.

'Forwards' means that place right between the feet, the natural bowing position. 'Backwards' means the opposite. If you are aiming for an *ikkyo* shape, aim to lead, or have *uke* fall forwards in his natural bowing position; if the result is a little left or right of that, so be it. Another very important point related to the twisting of the arm is that if one twists *uke*'s arm

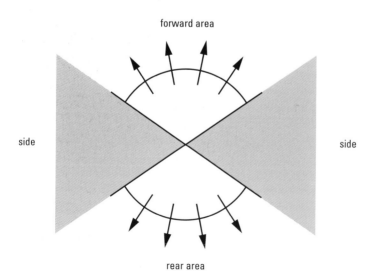

forward area

side

side

rear area

Two directions, to the front and to the rear.

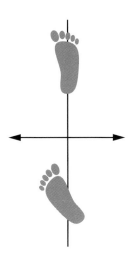

Weak line of balance in *hanmi* posture.

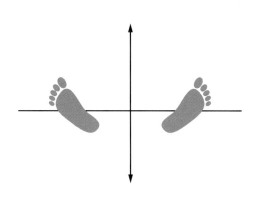

Weak line of balance in *shizen-hontai* posture.

inwards, he topples to the front; if it is turned outwards, he falls to the rear. This simple combination of twisting the arm and rear/forward movement covers almost every 'shape' in Aikido. It is a simple concept to grasp, and one that expands on knowledge better than trying to understand hundreds of seemingly spurious techniques.

Some Balance-Related Exercises

1. Have *uke* stand upright and tell him not to move. *Tori* grabs his lapel and draws him forward slowly. If *uke* truly does not want to move, he will come up on to the toes until he just has to take a step forwards. If *tori* pulls the left lapel, it will usually be with the left foot that *uke* steps, but not always. This is a useful beginning for learning Judo throws, and also offers the *aikidoka* an insight into balance. As *uke* begins to topple, *tori* moves in, drawing him on for a hip throw. Alternatively, *tori* could trip *uke* up when

off-balance and trying to step forwards, or *tori* could grab one lapel and one arm and perform a floating throw. If *uke* leans back too far, *tori* could take advantage and throw to the rear. This kind of training is rarely, if ever, done in Aikido, but is very useful.

Uke raising up on toes when pulled.

Uke cannot resist being pushed.

2. Have *uke* stand upright and tell him not to move. *Tori* walks behind *uke* and pushes *uke*'s head, slightly upwards. As above, *uke* has no choice but to rise up on the toes and eventually take a step. This provides useful insight into *iriminage*.

3. Make a circle with some belts and play Sumo. Whoever pushes *uke* out of the ring wins. But do they? *Uke* learns from this experience. As *uke* is pushed out, he gets the experience of what it is like to be on the edge. Quite often, in his desperation to remain in the ring, rather than simply be pushed out, he raises up a little becoming completely off-balance and open for a throw; perhaps he experiences that heart-stopping feeling of almost falling over a height. This explains why some of the throws in Sumo can be quite spectacular. After this experience of being on the edge, *uke* has gained an idea of what to aim to create when taking on the role of *tori*.

4. The art of the magician or pickpocket is to take the mind. The key to the art is distraction, which must be the most underdeveloped skill in Aikido. Have the students punch each other in the stomach. Anyone who has trained reasonably hard can take a half-decent blow to the stomach if prepared. Next, choose a student and ask him to relax his stomach completely. Feign a slow punch to his relaxed stomach – but do not hit! Even though there was no blow, he may feel a little queasy, simply at the thought of it. It would surely be possible to distract the mind of a mugger, for example, by holding some money out in one hand and leading them slightly forwards with it. Their stomach muscles would not be tense, not prepared, and you could take advantage of this and suddenly knock the wind out of them with even a gentle blow. Of course, there may be many other openings for attack. What is important is that, if *tori* can unbalance *uke* either physically or mentally, *uke* becomes momentarily so concerned with regaining his balance, perhaps even breathing in with shock, that he is

Distraction leads *uke* astray.

momentarily wide open for attack. One problem in Aikido is that at the point of breaking balance the aim is usually an immobilization or throw, which often takes too much time – the moment is over. A blow, at this moment, would have a far more debilitating effect, and perhaps at the same time enable the throw, or make it redundant.

5. *Tori* feigns an attack towards *uke*'s face. *Uke* flinches, moving his head rearwards. *Tori* follows up with *shomen-ate*.

6. *Tori* feigns an attack but *uke* blocks it by raising an arm. *Tori* makes contact, takes the arm and redirects according to *uke*'s response.

7. *Uke* grabs *tori*'s palm-up wrist strongly in *ai-hanmi*. *Tori* pushes towards *uke*'s centre gently until *tori* feels *uke* countering the action with force of his own. *Tori* turns slightly and rotates the hand palm-down, adds a little to that force, following it in its natural direction, and leads *uke* into a technique. From

an *ai-hanmi* grasp, *kote-gaeshi* is probably the easiest to do in this situation.

8. When *uke* grabs in *katate-dori*, *tori* makes a *shomen* strike to the head to distract *uke*, thereby causing uke momentarily to loosen his grip due to the change in focus. If *uke* continues to grab tightly, *tori* should consider hitting him for real!

9. A powerful short, sharp jerking force on one of *uke*'s arms can momentarily disorient them. It is not exactly traditional Aikido, but can prove very useful in self-defence.

10. Hit *uke*. Being struck is quite disorienting for most people. In Aikido, there are many feigning attacks, and the real hit is rarely carried home. You need not hit with a full hand; half should suffice for training.

11. Shout at *uke*. A loud *kiai* can be very effective at disorienting *uke* momentarily.

12. Have *uke* grasp *tori*'s hand violently, with speed and power. *Tori* receives it

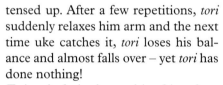

Uke pushes *tori's* left shoulder – gear cog movement.

Uke pushes *tori's* right shoulder – chain wheel movement.

tensed up. After a few repetitions, *tori* suddenly relaxes him arm and the next time uke catches it, *tori* loses his balance and almost falls over – yet *tori* has done nothing!

13. *Tori* and *uke* both stand in *shizen-hontai*. *Uke* takes a right step forwards and uses his right hand to push *tori's* right shoulder (or take the right hand). *Tori* retreats slightly and lures *uke* on. It looks like *ai-hanmi* for a moment, except *tori* steps back on the right side, effectively ending up in *gyaku-hanmi*. From here, the initial movement is like meshing gear cogs and a *tenkan* technique (*irimi-nage*) is natural. Next, using the same right hand, *uke* goes for *tori's* left side. This time, *tori* naturally steps back on his left side and what looked like a *gyaku-hanmi* beginning

ends up as *ai-hanmi* footwork. From here, the initial movement is like two chain wheels and, usually, an *irimi* technique (*shiho-nage*) is more natural than a *tenkan* one. Starting from *shizen-hontai* lures *uke* deeper into the attack and creates technique-specific *irimi* or *tenkan* shapes. This kind of stepping movement can be also practised to develop co-ordination and harmony. It is also very useful for studying the trips and reaps of Judo.

14. In Yoshinkan basics, *irimi* techniques are practised from *ai-hanmi*, *tenkan* from *gyakyu-hanmi*. While it is different to the mainstream Aikikai style, it is worth trying. For some techniques, it definitely makes more sense in the way certain 'shapes' unfold in terms of balance.

11 Generating Power

It may be that the race is not always to the swift, nor the battle to the strong – but that is the way to bet. *Damon Runyon*

The potential energy of movement is the latent energy that the practitioner has developed and stored in the body through training. It exists, waiting to be used. Once you begin to move, kinetic energy is created; the greater the mass that moves, and the greater the speed with which it moves, the more powerful will be that energy. The equation $KE=\frac{1}{2}MV^2$ shows that the speed component is of far more importance than the mass. This means that, with training, a smaller, yet faster person has every chance of out-performing a heavier, slower one. Learning to generate power does not mean performing hundreds of sit-ups, squats and press-ups. Instead, there are a number of methods by which you can develop and maintain an *aiki* kind of power in an *aiki* context; this is known as *kokyu-ryoku*.

For the weaker student, an external physical training programme may be useful. In this case, you need to be careful not to develop in an unbalanced way, or to train in such a way that *aiki* development is compromised.

Kokyu-Ryoku

Kokyu-ryoku is the strength behind solid *aiki*. It translates literally as 'breath power' but is better interpreted as being the clever co-ordination of breath and efficient body movement. Beginners often use brute strength to make technique but in time learn to use their body more efficiently.

But that does not mean less strength – continued practice makes the student stronger so that more *kokyu-ryoku* is available, yet increased skill means that less is used. Those who can do solid *kokyu-nage* against a madly resisting *uke* may be said to have good *kokyu-ryoku*. The whole point of it is to transfer this body-movement knowledge into ordinary Aikido techniques. If this can be done well, good, solid Aikido is the result.

Most practitioners try to develop *kokyu-ryoku* with *kokyu-ho*-type exercises. To develop powerful *kokyu-ryoku*, a resisting *uke* is your best friend. As *uke*, the student should learn to hold strongly yet without becoming too stiff or rigid; *tori* has to be careful not to become infected with *uke*'s apparent or real stiffness. The whole point is to be able to do it with seemingly little effort, paradoxically becoming quite strong in the process. The practitioner's *kokyu-ryoku* must be maintained at a reasonable level as the apparent lightness of Aikido is built on such power.

Body Movement

As a body art, Aikido has the potential to develop a significant amount of power. When moving from left to right, forwards and backwards, or diagonally, your body weight can be used to draw *uke* back and/or around centripetally, or to push them forwards and/or out centrifugally. These

Tori extends and moves well into *uke*'s space.

movements can be combined with upward or downward forces that further aid in causing *uke* to lose his centre of balance. All these movements are possible and, if you train with them in mind, the power within your technique can be developed rapidly.

In order to develop this power, you first need to get your co-ordination sorted out. To start, simply grasp a light *uke*'s sleeve and practise moving in the eight directions of avoidance, gently taking *uke* along for the ride. It is not wise to do this with power until the co-ordination is well established. Light practice is far better for developing co-ordination. Once the co-ordination is apparent, you can begin to practise with an *uke* who gives a heavier energy. *Uke* should not resist or struggle; he should just feel a little heavier.

Once you have developed the ability to use your body to develop even a modicum of power, appropriate care becomes necessary when applying ordinary techniques.

Moving from the Centre

All movement in Aikido begins in the body's centre. Being a body art, the body moves first, and the feet and hands follow. Aikido is a body art because it is based on movements of the Japanese sword. In contrast, the movement in rapier fencing originates in the hand, and the body and feet follow up. The difference lies in a combination of two factors: weight and killing method. While the Japanese sword is a heavier, cutting weapon, the rapier is a lighter, thrusting one. Although a Japanese sword is capable of the thrust, it is designed to cut strongly using both hands. This requires more strength, so the body needs to be behind the cut. The rapier, being light, is designed to be thrust with just one hand; as the hand can move more quickly than the body, that is where the movement originates, and the body follows.

It might be useful to draw an analogy with wrestling and boxing. A wrestler moves from the centre, while a boxer leads with the hands, and the good boxer times his short body movement to 'arrive' at the same time as his long reach.

It is not reasonable to say that either method is better, but you need to acknowledge the differences and respond accordingly when training. Knowing how your opponent moves ought to guide your training – knowledge is power.

One method to develop a feel for the body's centre is for *tori* and *uke* to push each other back and forth using their *tegatana*. Another method is for them both to place a *jo* down at their centre, pushing back and forth across the *tatami*. Increasing the resistance to the point that it just becomes a little difficult will help develop a feeling of moving from the centre and increase the student's ability in pushing from it. To push *uke* efficiently, drop a little lower and push up along the *jo*.

For self-practice, try making very short three-inch (8cm) Sumo-style *ayumi-ashi* steps and twisting the hips in co-ordination. Adding a modicum of power to the hip turn will, after time, create a direct link between the imaginary movement practised by the self and that done with a partner. Practising this same powerful walking movement while using the *bokken* or *jo* will aid in understanding the links between these seemingly separate arts.

In Judo, one trick to conserve energy is to push or drag *uke* around using his grip upon you. In Aikido grabbing attacks the feeling is the same. For example, from an *ushiro ryokata-dori* attack, *tori* performs *taisabaki* in such a way that *uke* is carried around by the transfer of momentum from *tori* to *uke*. In fact, twisting back and forth with *uke* clinging on behind is great practice to develop this kind of power and the principle learned can be used in many techniques. It can also be practised while raising the *bokken*, real or imaginary, in the *hasso* style, first to the left, then to the right, and so on.

Torifune

Torifune is an excellent method for developing power in the forward and rearward directions. Standing in a half horse-stance with feet straight ahead, moving from left to right gives a lateral version of *torifune* that is indispensable for developing power when moving to the left or right. Stepping diagonally, you have the choice between the more forward *torifune*, or the more lateral horse-stance movement.

When moving back and forth in *torifune*, or from side to side in a horse-stance, it makes sense to keep the feet at a distance that allows an easy transfer of one hundred per cent of the weight from one to the other. Although wide stances are good for flexibility training, if the feet are too far

Unbendable arm position.

apart in Aikido exercises, rapid movement becomes awkward. You need to be able to push or draw with full power and to be able to move around at the same time. The feeling in the feet should be one of grabbing the *tatami* with the toes.

The Arms

Unbendable Arm

The principle of the unbendable arm is a key element in Aikido training. Although it is often viewed as being nothing more than a cheap trick, in fact it is a very real trick, and the principle can be put to good use in your techniques. An almost extended arm is very powerful; keeping it extended will aid in directing *uke* to the ground.

When learning about the unbendable arm, students seem to fall into two categories: those who can do it immediately, and those who struggle for years before it slowly clicks. It does not seem to be something that can be easily taught; instead, the student needs to figure it out for himself. One trick that might help is to get into a press-up position with arms slightly curved, not locked out, and work on the feel. 'Remember' the way the muscles in the arms 'are' and try to replicate that feeling when standing.

When the arm is 'energized' it becomes unbendable. It cannot be easily bent, nor easily straightened. This of course needs to be taken into account when performing techniques, since both *tori* and *uke* are likely to be of an unbendable *aiki* nature. It is essential to find a way around it so that, rather than bending, you lead.

In the same way as the unbendable arm, when one 'energizes' the stomach or hip area, the region between the lower and upper body becomes unbendable. If you can 'energize' the link between the arm and the hand – the wrist – it, too, will become unbendable, and it will be difficult for that wrist to be twisted. Finally, when practising counters, maintaining a 'flexible unbendability' will help in preventing your partner from making the technique, and enable smooth transition to the counter.

Heaviness

Power in Aikido comes from having heavy arms. In *kokyu-ho*, the palm-up heavy arm is often used, in *irimi-nage*, it is the thumb-down heavy arm. There are four types that need to be developed: palm-up, thumb-up, palm-down and thumb-down. Here, the arms are extended in four different forms, and since all of these forms are extant in Aikido techniques, the practitioner ought to develop a heavy arm for each one. Also, if there is a heavy arm, so must there be a heavy leg, and a heavy body. A proficient groundwork technician in Judo will always have mastered the art of the heavy body. With hardly any effort, they melt into and crush their opponent so that they cannot move, or, in some cases,

even breathe. In Aikido, lowering the body's centre while performing critical parts of techniques will help develop a heavier body.

Extended Arms

The idea of extending the arms is similar to that of the unbendable arm but far easier to put into practice. You need to forget about the arm being unbendable, and concentrate instead on reaching and extending, as if trying to touch the ceiling. First, practise extending the arms up towards the ceiling, out towards the front or side, and down to the floor as strongly as possible. Next, remember that feeling in the arms while trying a few techniques. Finally, try again, using less energy. Starting with a lot of energy and slowly reducing it to the amount necessary to perform the technique offers a means to develop the skill. This feeling of extension can also be used to hone your strikes.

Heavy arm at work.

Tension

Tension exercises can be divided into dynamic and natural. In dynamic tension exercises, you strain the muscles to their fullest extent while moving slowly from position to position as in, say, a Kung Fu pattern. The key is to maintain as much tension as possible and the benefit is that it combines an element of martial co-ordination with strength exercises.

Natural tension exercises are commonly performed without moving. You simply maintain a certain posture for a time from one to five minutes, or more. Such exercises are 'natural' in the sense that no tension is demanded of the student, yet, simply holding the position for sustained periods can be very strenuous and thus tension develops naturally as time passes.

Maintaining a static position develops natural tension.

Pressing the *jo* to develop natural tension.

The positions adopted typically resemble certain martial stances and both dynamic and natural tension exercises train muscle groups to reform themselves to the extent that the student begins to feel more comfortable performing these postures or patterns. While not of Aikido in origin, both these types of training can provide benefits.

Turning

Turning movements, or *taisabaki*, are done in two distinguishing ways. One school of thought sweeps the rear leg around in a large arc, in the other the rear foot steps straight back. Sweeping the leg around in a large arc adds power to the technique in a broad way and is useful for trips and sweeps. Stepping back is faster and focuses on the pivot.

When performing a *taisabaki* movement such as *tenkan* it is often to avoid an attack but, with a little thought and practice, a lot of power can be generated by this exercise. Combining the straight and lateral *torifune* creates a kind of circular one, whereby *taisabaki* and *torifune* are combined, which becomes more effective in breaking balance the closer your centre gets to the target point on *uke*'s body – the head as in *irimi-nage*, the elbow as in *juji-nage*, or the wrist as in *kote-gaeshi*.

When you are watching powerful performers of these techniques, you will notice two types. The first type moves in behind *uke* and spins round quickly maintaining a forward stance. He sometimes turns all the way around, dropping to one knee; it is similar to a *torifune*-type movement with the inclusion of lowering his centre deeply. The second type spins in the same way but uses a more lateral horse-stance type of movement, again dropping the centre, but more slightly. Both of these movements draw *uke* in using centripetal

force. Once *tori* begins to make technique, *uke* is typically thrown off with centrifugal force. Sometimes, though, *uke* is drawn in so strongly that the centripetal force alone is enough to take them to the floor.

Naturally, the wise student ought to think hard of exercises that could develop his centripetal or centrifugal power. One idea is to imagine tight elastic wrapping around the waist as you turn. In this way, you can turn with dynamic power, even when training alone.

Grips

Yonkyo *Grip*

Aikidoka usually develop a powerful grip. To make the grip more uniform, to make it a principle, it is useful to think of *yonkyo*. In *yonkyo*, the inner knuckle of the index finger is pressed against *uke*'s arm, causing pain. Holding firmly with the lower fingers, the index finger is free to point. It is not easy to perform well and needs constant development. Often, people with small bony hands are better at it than those with a more bear-like structure.

In order to develop the *yonkyo* grip it is a good idea to make all of your grips in the *yonkyo* fashion. For instance, use a *yonkyo* grip when holding *katate-dori* as *uke*, when making *ikkyo* as *tori*, when holding the *bokken* or *jo*, and even when holding the hand rail while standing on a train. In particular, it is quite enlightening to use the *yonkyo* grip while making techniques. It does not have to cause any pain, it just helps make good technique. It is a solid principle. It stands to reason then that *tori* should learns to avoid the power of *uke*'s *yonkyo* grip.

Hasso *Grip*

There are two ways to hold the sword in *hasso* posture. One method, the most common, is to stand in *hasso* posture with the

Hasso posture, elbows down.

Hasso posture, elbows extended.

left foot forwards, sword hilt at the shoulder, sword pointing up, with the elbows down, half-relaxed. Carefully consider the position of the elbows. In this case it allows for relaxed, fast cutting and no one would deny it is conductive to good *aiki* training. The second method is to stand in the same *hasso* position but with the elbows splayed up and outwards horizontally, infused with energy. Here, it is useful to stretch the sword hilt somewhat between the two hands while holding it, thereby adding to that splayed-out feeling. Also, when cutting, try to maintain that splayed-out feeling in the arms even though, by necessity, they come together somewhat as the sword descends. Even at the bottom of the cut, they remain slightly splayed out, still stretching the hilt. This style of grip can be used for *shomen-uchi*, *yokomen-uchi* and *tsuki* and offers insight into swordwork that leads directly to empty-hand techniques.

One particular exercise will explain this in more detail. Have two people try to pull your arms apart from the elbows, one on

Tori can meet, hit, cut or push.

Ai-hanmi – striking the attacking arm.

either side, while touching your fingers together about a foot (30cm) from the centre of your chest. It is quite easy to stop them pulling your arms apart; in fact, if you let them pull your arms apart a little, you can easily draw them back to the centre. It is a very efficient position. Now, as they continue to pull, try to remember the feeling in your chest/abdomen area and which muscles are being energized. Think of it as an extension of the unbendable arm idea.

Next, ask your partners to let go, but maintain the feeling and pick up the sword, taking *hasso* posture. Now it will feel like a very powerful posture. Finally, put down the sword, and try *irimi-nage*, keeping that same energy in your arms and chest.

Try a few different techniques and you might have another of those mini-enlightenments. This does not mean that you abandon a previous approach, merely that you have a new one to consider.

Hitting and Cutting

Aikidoka often make a cutting movement with the hand, or *tegatana* (hand-sword), during techniques. It can be a soft meeting of arms, it can be a hit, and it can be a cut. By far the most common is the soft meeting of arms in harmony. 'Hitting' means attacking the other's weapon (arm) by hitting it. If *uke* had a knife, then the shock or pain of the strike might cause it to be dropped. 'Cutting' means adding considerable weight and following through, or pressing. You could also hit and then cut.

It may sound odd, but, when break-falling in Aikido, every time you whack the mat hard with an arm you are potentially practising a hit. Accordingly, hitting the mat hard after a break-fall can be useful. To develop this as an independent skill or to raise awareness of its potential, from standing drop to one knee and whack the mat with your forearm. After doing this for about a minute, try doing *irimi-nage*. It is enlightening and you may well walk the streets with more quiet confidence afterwards.

Winding the Bobbin

Hold one end of a belt in the hand and wind it rapidly around the wrist. Here, both wrists turn in circles, one much bigger than the other and it is exactly this

Rapidly winding a belt around the wrist provides insight into *ikkyo* movement.

A sharp jerk can disorient *uke*.

A sharp parry.

movement that is the source of power in many techniques starting with *ikkyo* and ending with *bokken* or *jo*. Work this movement into your techniques – no one will ever show you.

Jerking

A jerk can be a short sharp pull or a short sharp push. They are not common in Aikido, but they are the kind of movements that can turn tame Aikido into effective self-defence. Significantly, a sharp jerk can disorient an aggressor quite severely, allowing you either to follow up with another technique, or to get away.

To develop the power in your jerking movement you need a very agreeable *uke*. When jerking the arm downwards it is important for *uke* to know in advance, so that he can stiffen up his neck muscles slightly to avoid whiplash. A little practice will establish a powerful jerk, and that power will increase four-fold if your body weight is behind it, especially in combination with the stomach crunch (*see* below).

Another use of a jerking motion is in parrying or blocking an attack. As an attack comes, say, a *yokomen-uchi*, your arm meets it in the ordinary way but, at the point of contact, a short, sharp strike is delivered with the side of the forearm. This can be likened to hitting or cutting the arm with a chopping knife. From a distance it looks like a Karate block but is in fact a hit that fits the movement in space and time. This 'counter-strike' can blend with the attack, it can be either a defensive or attacking parry, or it can simply be an effective straight block. A small jerking movement can also be used to push uke away to great effect. After a lot of practice the rough edges of a jerk can be smoothed out until it looks more like a strong pull or push.

Crunching

Strong stomach muscles allow the erect body to crunch downwards slightly with great force. With *uke* in your grasp, by forcefully bending down slightly, or crunching, a strong off-balancing movement can be made. Here, the stomach muscles are being used to draw *uke* forwards; it is not quite Aikido in style, but it is very effective in result. Similarly, straightening up after a crunch offers more power for use in the technique.

If you crunch slightly to the left or right, this has the effect of drawing *uke* around centripetally. This is not quite the same as lowering your centre, which can achieve the same result. Lowering your centre while holding *uke* has the effect of adding your body weight to the point of contact; if that point of contact is within a technique, such as *nikyo*, or strikes a pressure point, so much the better. Of course, lowering your centre and crunching can be done at the same time.

Jumping

Often seen in Ki Aikido classes, jumping can be analysed in two parts. First, by jumping, *tori* can move in quickly behind *uke* for *tenkan*. Here, the increased momentum given by the speed of the jump is used to draw *uke* around using centripetal force. Second, since what goes up must come down, *tori* can also develop extra power to the technique by dropping heavily. The most important point in jumping is timing the movement to coincide with *uke*'s attack and matching it to an appropriate technique.

Vigorous Training

If you train to develop power yet never use it, how will you know how to put it in the technique? You need to train hard. Vigorous training means *uke* gets up and attacks immediately, repeatedly. When you have trained hard for a period of time, it is possible to train lightly yet with intensity. *Uke* also needs to strike strongly, just enough to push *tori*. When gripping, *uke* should grip hard enough to give *tori* something to work with to overcome. Sometimes *tori* may fail to do the technique. That gives him something to work on. In this way, you will be able to train ever harder and develop real skill.

It is not easy to do it the other way around. For example, if you only trained lightly and *uke* just flew, you would not be familiar with the difference between correct and incorrect movement. After training hard against a measure of resistance, you know where to move, and training lightly can then, and only then, be done correctly. Of course, it is also essential to train lightly, as this encourages speed and aids co-ordination, timing, balance and centre. *Uke* learns how to become fast yet heavy at the same time; *tori* learns how to deal with it.

Your goal should always be to mix the two extremes, and to be able to deal with a heavy, uncooperative *uke* in a light manner. It goes without saying that this should be done in a friendly way and not become overly competitive.

When to Use Power

The physical power developed during Aikido training needs to be focused in breaking *uke*'s balance, either physically, mentally, or both, and taking advantage of it by being in the right place at the right time and making clean technique. You need to develop your *aiki* power as a martial artist but, as your technical skill increases, you will not be able to use it to the full without injuring *uke*. *Kokyu-nage* techniques, however, allow you to practise hard in safety. There are no locks or twisted joints to damage and practice is limited by the extent to which both partners want to do it, since the training must be equal – you cannot slam *uke* into the mat and expect anything but that in return. Training may be gentle or vigorous, but there must be a negotiated pact between *tori* and *uke*. If you want to train gently, throw *uke* gently. More importantly, the hardest part of any technique is the beginning and this is where you need to give most attention. It is bad form to receive a slow attack only to finish up slamming *uke* down into the mat at that vulnerable last moment when he has placed his body under your complete trust.

12 Principles

Things should be made as simple as possible, but not any simpler. *Albert Einstein*

It is the principles that students should be searching for; they are the same in each art. No art has a monopoly on the principles, although certain arts might be said to emphasize certain principles. The principles determine the form, of which there are many variations. It is therefore strange that it is usually the forms that determine the art. This has to be a mistake. If the principles are targeted, then there can be no determining the forms. If you search for the principles, and come to understand them, your forms will be limitless.

From Technique to Principle

For some, Aikido techniques are principles in themselves; this cannot be argued, but it is also possible to look for principles within the techniques. A principle is a common movement, shape, or feeling discernible across a range of techniques. To learn Aikido efficiently it is useful to identify certain common principles, collect them, study them, test them, and apply them. In the broad sense, *ikkyo*, the well-known first technique of Aikido, could be a principle, but here, as it is *ikkyo* itself that proves so difficult to fathom, it is worth isolating individual instances within the *ikkyo* movement for individual scrutiny.

Perhaps the initial entry movement of a certain teacher is isolated. The movement is common to many other techniques and is therefore a principle. Practising the movement many times by yourself leads you along a voyage of discovery. At first, the movement seems simple, yet, after careful scrutiny, many subtle variations in foot, hip and hand positions can be discerned that potentially produce slight variations in technique, or *henka-waza*. A variation ought by definition to be a different, yet acceptable approach to any movement. These same variations in movement can then be applied in other techniques. When watching, it is often not easy to see such subtle differences – they need to be felt.

Principles can relate to footwork, hip movements, body movements, twists, postures, directions, and so on. Another example is time: when performing *ikkyo* from *shomen-uchi*; you could cut at the same time; you could cut earlier than *uke*; you could cut after *uke*; or you could start late but overtake *uke*. As to how early or how late, if *uke*'s up and down striking motion comprises a 360-degree cycle then *tori*'s response can be rationalized as being, say, 90 or 180 degrees late, for example. In terms of power: you could cut with the same strength as *uke*, more strongly than *uke*, or more softly than *uke*. At first, the best practice is to cut at the same time and be of equal power. Harmony comes first but after much practice you will then be able to change the time, or power. Without harmony there are no options from which

Lines indicate possible
directions of movement.

A   *sankyo*
B   *sumi-otashi*
C   *shiho-nage tenkan*
D   *kate-gaeshi*
E   *udekime-nage*
F   *shiho-nage*

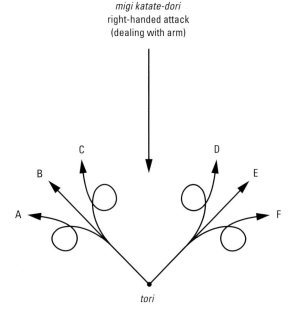

migi katate-dori
right-handed attack
(dealing with arm)

tori

to begin, just chaos. In grabbing, *uke* typically grasps strongly and *tori* reacts strongly. Both are equal in the beginning but, with practice, *tori* learns to respond softly, ignoring *uke*'s apparent hardness and not becoming infected by it.

These ideas are applicable to all the techniques. Outlines of some of the more broader principles are given below. Other more specific principles are located elsewhere, throughout the text.

From Principle to Technique

Starting from *ai-hanmi* (or *gyaku-hanmi katate-dori*), entering to the front for *irimi*, *tori* has the choice of turning clockwise or anti-clockwise, resulting in two different techniques. Entering to the rear, *tori*'s hips can likewise turn either way, resulting in two more different techniques. Such a way of analysing the situation can make otherwise separate-looking techniques appear to follow simple easy-to-learn rules of contrasting movement. In this case, there are

two movements to the front and two to the rear, making a total of four. From these four initial principles a great many basic Aikido techniques begin. Of course, *tori* might decide not to turn at all while entering, producing a further two 'direct' entry movements.

Recognition of Shapes

Once past the basics, in order to escape the rigidity of the form it is better to refer to the techniques as shapes. Viewing the techniques as shapes allows for more variation in technique but, more importantly, this principle aims at recognizing a shape in *uke* that is waiting to be acted upon in the moment. A higher skill is in predicting the shape that *uke* will present, that is, where *uke* will be a short moment in the future. Another method is to create the shape that *uke* presents either by luring *uke* this way or that, or feigning attack, causing *uke* to respond in a predicted manner. To take maximum advantage, the important thing is to be in the right place when *uke* arrives. Meeting at the same time creates the best harmony.

Referring to a technique with the more flexible concept of 'shape' will help, since it suggests that variation from the norm, or experimentation, is acceptable.

Kokyu

Aiki typically first manifests itself in *kokyu-ho* and *kokyu-nage* practice. Good *aiki* transcends the technical and is what the practitioner feels when the *kokyu* techniques are performed well. Later, it will transfer over to the techniques and will be felt by a perceptive *tori* or *uke*. *Kokyu* exercises isolate technical detail and focus on simple body movement. When performing these exercises it is especially important to be in good posture and to have 50 per cent of your energy in each hand. If that 50 per cent can be maintained even though the hand is empty, then it will help with balance, breathing and co-ordination.

Three teachers might typically do any *kokyu-ho* or *kokyu-nage* in three different ways in terms of footwork and hand/hip positions. If the simplest of movements have variations, then it follows that those same three teachers will do *ikkyo* or *irimi-nage* slightly differently, and that these three variations might be explained according to the three different ways they do *kokyu-nage*. The wise student will isolate parts of the movement and be able to distinguish between them, or demonstrate several variations, whereas the ordinary student will have just one method and never question it, nor will he notice any differences. Even if he does, he will probably think it to be wrong.

If you are stuck within a particular technique, find a corresponding *kokyu-nage* and practise it instead; it will probably provide the answer. *Kokyu* movements are great principles so collect as many as possible, but without insisting that they be set in stone.

Tenkan-Ho

This simple turning exercise bores and confuses many, but it holds the key to Aikido. *Uke* should hold firmly, perhaps imagining pressing a coin against *tori*'s wrist while pressing in slightly towards *tori*'s centre signifying attack. Even when *tori* moves, the grip must be maintained in such a way that the coin does not fall. By necessity, *uke* must move his centre forward to maintain the constant 'contact' of attack. *Tori* does not drag *uke* around. Far from it – *uke* attacks and follows *tori* as *tori* evades. Nor is it good practice to swing *uke* 180 degrees around to the front. Keep *uke* at the side, blocking his entry with careful body positioning. From here, *tori* can push or project *uke* around to the front and start again. Also, *tori* should make sure that *uke* is able maintain a comfortable grip; if *uke* is forced to let go, then he will, of necessity, let go and renew the attack. If *uke*'s grip is too strong, you need to examine the arm positions, being cautious not to struggle directly against *uke*'s *yonkyo* grip, for example.

Offering the hand palm-down is one method that helps *tori* tremendously. Starting palm-down, move the body weight forward, placing your own elbow almost over *uke*'s, but ever so slightly to the outside. At the same time, curl the wrist palm-up in the direction of *uke*'s attack towards your own centre. Move slightly to the side and step just behind *uke*'s leading foot and finish by extending both arms equally, as though holding a large ball. Extending unequally will tend to leave *tori* off-balance – the ball will drop.

In another method, *tori* offers the hand to *uke* with the palm sideways, or

Tenkan-ho from the front.

Tenkan-ho from the side.

thumb-up. From this position *tori* again steps slightly sideways and to *uke*'s rear but this time makes a very small *yokomen*-type movement with the grasped hand. Naturally, it makes sense to practise *katate-dori kokyu-ho* from various other positions, such as from behind, or with the hand thrust upwards in a *sankyo*-like position, and so on.

Unfortunately, a great many *aikidoka* forget what they have learned in *tenkan-ho* when practising the techniques. With a good understanding of *tenkan-ho*, the student ought to be able to do any *katate-dori* or *ryote-dori* technique with ease, no matter what gorilla is hanging on the end of his arm. If it cannot be done, the student should go back to *tenkan-ho*. A good place

to start to apply *tenkan-ho* in a technique is to investigate and modify the movement of the lower hand of *tenchi-nage*. Instead of just thrusting straight down to *uke*'s rear corner, try beginning with a tiny circle as in *tenkan-ho* before the thrust. After such practice, the straight thrust becomes almost redundant.

Suwari-Waza Kokyu-Ho

This exercise proves quite difficult for many. As in the *tenkan-ho* exercise from standing, the lesson learned here translates into a broader understanding of how to do Aikido techniques with more finesse. Simple, solid *suwari-waza kokyu-ho* represents good Aikido. Standard practice is for *tori* to work the hands inside of *uke*'s arms

The principle of *tenkan-ho* can be used in many situations – note the bottom hand.

pushing both hands up, or one up and one down. *Tori* can also work outside *uke*'s arms, or cross them. Sometimes, *tori* uses a very strong push to develop strong *kokyu-ryoku*; this is the less harmonic approach. Here, *uke* struggles to maintain his grip; some criticize this as being non-*aiki* in approach but such practice is essential as, if done well enough, it teaches control of the extent of *uke*'s grip. At the other end of the spectrum the aim is to lead *uke* in such a way that he maintains a comfortable grip. Both these extremes form an essential part of the whole and, once acquired, naturally transfer over into the standard *waza*.

Using two hands in *suwari-waza kokyu-ho* is obviously more difficult to synchronize so students must vary the practice between light and heavy. If 'x' defines *tori*'s ability then *uke* needs to recognize that and grip just enough to help *tori* go for 'x+1'. It is a co-operative learning process, not a competition of strength. Viewing *suwari-waza kokyu-ho* as just another exercise or just another technique will deprive the student of perhaps the best means of understanding Aikido.

Irimi and *Tenkan* Rationale

The ideas of *irimi* and *tenkan* (or *omote* and *ura*) can be explained in several ways, all of them being legitimate in terms of principles that can be carried over to other techniques:

1. *Irimi* is seen as entering *uke*'s attack and the entrance is made across *uke*'s front side. *Tenkan* is made to the rear, across *uke*'s closed side. Simply, entering to the front or rear gives two different variations of any technique and this is the way most Aikikai schools follow, performing two *irimi*, and two *tenkan* variations for each technique.

2. An *irimi* variation is seen as returning *uke*'s energy back from whence it came – back towards *uke*; contrasting this, *tenkan* is the opposite, allowing *uke*'s energy to continue on along its original line of attack.

3. The two are differentiated by *uke*'s action. If *uke* grabs and pulls, then *tori* does an *irimi* technique; if *uke* pushes, *tori* performs *tenkan*. Contrasting this completely, an advanced *aikidoka* can pull when pulled and push when pushed.

4. The push/pull idea is limited to attacks made in *ai-hanmi* and *gyakyu-hanmi* respectively. In *ai-hanmi*, *uke* pulls and *tori* makes an *irimi* movement; conversely, from *gyakyu-hanmi*, *uke* pushes and *tori* makes a *tenkan* technique.

5. If *tori* responds to *uke*'s attack early then *tori* rushes in making an *irimi* technique; if late, a *tenkan* movement suffices.

6. *Tori* initiates for *irimi* techniques, and *uke* initiates for *tenkan* techniques. Yoshinkan Aikido follows this principle and extends it so that *ai-hanmi* is the preferred starting point for *irimi*, and *gyakku-hanmi* for *tenkan* techniques. For example, *ai-hanmi shomen-uchi ikkyo* (*ikajo*) would see *tori* (otherwise referred to as *shite* in Yoshinkan) initiating the attack and performing *ikkyo* (*ikajo*). The first three techniques of the *Koryu Dai Ichi kata* of Shodokan Aikido also show this. In the first technique, *tori* attacks *shomen-uchi* and makes *shomen-uchi ikkyo irimi* (*oshi-taoshi*). In the second technique, *uke* attacks *shomen-uchi* and *tori* performs *ikkyo tenkan* (*tentai oshi-taioshi*). In the third technique, both *tori* and *uke* attack simultaneously, in harmony, and *tenkan yonkyo* (*tekubi-osae*) is the result.

7. *Tori* always aims to make an *irimi* technique, *tenkan* is the result if too much resistance is met. Accordingly, some even insist that there is no such thing as *tenkan*.

8. As seen in Kyushido, *tori* and *uke* start from *shizen-hontai*. To take *migi ai-hanmi*, *uke* must make a step forwards. However, as *uke* grabs, *tori* steps back with the right leg and the result is *gyaku-hanmi* in terms of the feet. The technique that fits this position is usually a *tenkan* variation. Also, when *uke* tries to take *gyaku-hanmi*, *tori* steps back and an *ai-hanmi* foot position is the result. From here, an *irimi* technique often works best. From this, it is clear that it is the foot rather than the hand positions that give meaning to *ai-hanmi* or *gyakyu-hanmi*.

9. No matter whether you start in *ai-hanmi*, *gyaku-hanmi* or *shizen-hontai*, in most schools it is the norm for *irimi* techniques to originate from an *ai-hanmi*-style entrance; *tenkan* techniques generally require a *gyaku-hanmi* entrance, although it is also possible to do exactly the opposite on occasion.

10. Finally, some schools, such as Shodo-kan Aikido and Takeda-ryu Aikido, do not really teach in terms of making such strong distinctions between *irimi* and *tenkan*.

To an observer all these differences might add up to the same thing, but the way the student rationalizes it in the mind reflects the kind of Aikido that is produced. Rather than the essence of *aiki* being different, the above are differences in style, or learning method. Each of the above is a legitimate principle in various schools; all, from principle to no-principle, can be used as independent principles in any student's training. It is certainly valuable for the curious student to experiment with variations not found in his own art.

Sokumen

Sokumen means 'side entry' and appears to fit midway between *irimi* and *tenkan* movements. In basic *sokumen*, the practitioner typically ends up in a position at an angle of 90 degrees to *uke*'s line of attack, but in practice it can vary considerably. Few schools use it, and even fewer adopt it as a principle that can be used in other common techniques from *ikkyo* to *kote gaeshi*, and so on.

One important distinction is that, from a *sokumen* entry, *tori* often has the option of going for either an *irimi* or *tenkan* movement – it is a central position, or junction (*see* below). For example, when doing *sokumen irimi-nage*, at the central point of balance-taking, take a pause, and examine how you could throw either forwards or backwards, or change to different *waza* such as *ikkyo* or *shiho-nage*. *Sokumen* is subtle, quick and safe. *Tori* evades and is in a position to respond immediately. It is an excellent position which is extremely useful in more practical applications, especially against punches and kicks and for general self-defence. Frankly, it should be used more. It is a great principle.

Junctions

Midway through many movements, it is possible to find common junctions that link techniques. Rather than just sailing through a particular technique, it is important to pause and ponder at these junctions. If you simply do *shomen-uchi ikkyo* from beginning to end with no other thought, the point will be completely missed. The initial avoidance creates a junction; the initial meeting creates a junction; the cut-down creates a junction. Learn to recognize and create junctions,

Sokumen entrance is from the side.

from which you can either do the required technique as being taught by the teacher, or switch to another.

Symmetry of Techniques

The techniques correspond to each other in terms of symmetry and this principle is very useful in developing combinations. For example, if *uke*'s right arm rushes forwards and you receive it in right posture and rotate it clockwise, then you may end up with *ikkyo*; if it were a left, you might end up with *kote-gaeshi*, or *shiho-nage*. If there were no resistance to these initial moves, then the technique would be carried through to completion. If *uke* suddenly began to resist and get up, the

ikkyo might be switched to *irimi-nage*; the *kote-gaeshi* could be quickly switched to *shomen-ate*.

There are many possibilities and it depends upon where you are in relation to *uke* and what 'shape' you recognize in the moment. Here, the principle is to rotate to the right, the technique being determined by what *uke* does next. This is possible due to the inherent symmetry between techniques. Also, in terms of counters, you need look no further than your own hands. We often twist our own hands or arms to their extreme in the process of making technique and, accordingly, there are many opportunities waiting to be taken by a smart *uke*.

Arms and Hands

Arm Shapes

Uke's arm typically presents itself in four positions: palm-up, thumb-up, palm-down and thumb-down. One more position is palm-up at the opposite extreme, forming an *ude-gatame* shape. It is unlikely that *uke* would present *tori* with such a shape, as it would be too obvious an opportunity, but the shape does exist, waiting to be created. If *tori* can distinguish between the shapes as presented by *uke* as they approach, a suitable technique can be applied accordingly.

Equal Hands

It is important to have equal energy in each hand. When doing techniques, if *tori* has more energy in one hand than the other when pushing, he may twist too far and/or become slightly off-balance. Accordingly, though one hand is empty, both should still be extended equally, and this principle should be applied to all techniques. In Judo, one principle is to attack the weak side of the body. If you feel that the opponent has too much energy extending from his right side, you should immediately attack the left, as it is vulnerable.

The Magic of Three

Many movements can be rationalized in terms of three. Arms, legs, hips and head rotate either to the left or right, or remain at a neutral point in the middle. When thrusting with the sword, the blade can be straight, twisted to the left, or twisted to the right. Timing can be early, in harmony, or late. Techniques can be done in terms of *jodan*, *chudan* and *gedan*. Breathing can be relaxed, focused or in the form of *kiai*. Striking can be hit-and-retreat, hit-and-transfer momentum, or hit-and-follow-through. *Tori* can immobilize *uke*, *tori* can

project *uke*, or *tori* can let *uke* escape. *Tori* can push, draw or deal with *uke* on the spot. *Tori* can perform most of the movement, *tori* can stand somewhat still and make *uke* do most of the moving, or both *tori* and *uke* can move somewhat equally. In space, *uke* can be in front, to the side or to the rear. When *tori* moves with respect to *uke*, the movement can be analysed as turning like two meshing cogs or gears, or turning like a chain on two sprockets, or linearly. It is possible to dissect movement in this way and it helps in analysing technique in the midst of movement.

In rationalizing movements like this it becomes clear that when performing, say, a right-handed *ikkyo* or *irimi-nage*, the hips, arms and legs are all generally moving clockwise at the moment of contact. Being aware of how you move makes it easier to see what the teacher is doing. It also becomes easier to discover variations that follow Aikido principles.

Immobilizations

All five basic immobilizations follow the path of *ikkyo* and controlling the elbow is a key element in each. For example, when taking *nikyo*, try to guide *uke*'s elbow through a similar trajectory to *ikkyo*. The same can be said of *sankyo*, *yonkyo* and *gokyo*. In *irimi* techniques, you must be careful not to give *uke*'s energy directly back to him, otherwise it may result in a clash and/or *uke* will regain composure.

Some schools have a sixth immobilization, *rokkyo*, otherwise known as *waki-gatame* (an armlock more common in Judo), a devastatingly useful technique that can be done almost instantaneously when any of the basic five fail to work. Armlocks are often frowned upon in Aikido but they can be done by extending rather than locking, thereby making them more acceptable to the doubters. In fact, doing it in this way allows the practitioner to add far more power safely – always good practice for self-defence. One simpler armlock is *ude-gatame*, sometimes known as *ude-hishigi*. Interestingly, for effective armlocks, it is necessary to find the path of most resistance in order to apply pain.

Projections

In projecting, *uke* flies off at a tangent centrifugally. Getting rid of *uke* in this way allows faster practice, as in *ninin-dori*. Of course, it is possible to throw down centripetally as in Judo, but then it is necessary to keep the attention right there and immobilize since *uke* would be dangerously close. When projecting with the *jo*, push along its length; if you bend the *jo* too much, it will break. When projecting with *kokyu-nage*, the arm works in just the same way.

After throwing, your posture can be either forward or central. Do not simply let it happen; make a rational choice and practise both, so that your posture ends up forward or central because you wanted it to.

Still Techniques

Most people have a mental picture of the direction in which they should move in relation to *uke*. In basic technique, it is *tori* who does most of the moving. Practising without moving the body adds another dimension. Try sitting in *seiza* or standing in *shizen-hontai* and let *uke* take your wrist from the side as in *gyaku-hanmi*. Rock towards *uke* slightly, making contact, and then drop back, drawing *uke*'s hand in front while sending him behind as in *shiho-nage*, then bring him all the way around to your front and throw. This is *shiho-nage*, yet *tori* has hardly moved. Trying it again from *ai-hanmi* produces *ikkyo*.

Although these are not really practical as techniques, this kind of practice helps

develop *aiki*. It is also good preparation for understanding the more realistic situation, in which both *tori* and *uke* move around in unison as the technique unfolds – midway along the continuum.

One Technique

The concept of 'one technique' being used to incapacitate *uke* is prevalent in Aikido, even if it is not clearly stated. Here, *uke*'s attack is so determined that *tori* can easily produce a single technique to deal with it. Accordingly, many (if not most) schools train to deal with a single, clearly defined attack with the idea that one technique controls it. The majority of training time, sometimes years, is spent trying to figure out how to refine such perfect technique until it works. In concept, it is quite a realistic and necessary principle to aim for, but, in practice, it fails to prepare for a more cautious *uke* who does not overcommit. The overbearing idea of 'one technique' explains why, in Aikido, few combinations are taught in any structured fashion. It makes sense to be aware of such limitation.

Displacing *uke*

When performing *kokyu-nage* it is useful to take *uke*'s place. For example, when projecting, as in *morote-dori kokyu-nage*, as you step forward to throw, move the hips slightly into *uke*'s space, and the feet follow. As *uke* disappears, you assume his previous space – you have displaced *uke* from his spot. This has the effect of making the projection slightly spiral in nature and is also excellent entering practice for *koshi-nage*. Having displaced *uke* many times in *kokyu-nage*, the student will soon realize that it is possible to perform a similar movement in, say, *irimi-nage*, or *tenchi-nage*.

With a little imagination, this principle – the feeling of displacement – can be applied in most other techniques, even *ikkyo*. On acquiring this principle, entering further still, a whole new range of koshi-nage-type techniques will emerge, such as *ikkyo koshi-nage*.

Kuzushi and *Tsukuri*

Common in Judo or Shodokan Aikido, the terms *kuzushi* and *tsukuri* – relating to breaking balance before making technique – are seldom heard in the more 'traditional' forms of Aikido. Of course, the balance must always be broken but in sport styles it is more important, otherwise you will never be able to throw a resisting opponent. In the traditional styles it is *uke*'s zealous, singular, committed attack that is used. Here, *uke* may even overextend, off-balancing himself. This is intended to match the kind of outright committed attack that might occur on the battlefield.

Hard or Soft

A common analogy of *ki* is water coming from a hose. Whether it comes out under high or low pressure, its essence remains unchanged – it is still water. The skill then is to be able to increase or decrease your pressure, or energy, while maintaining essence, or flexibility. Some people insist on always working only at low pressure, others only at high pressure, but this kind of approach restricts development. A runner sometimes runs slowly and sometimes fast. His aim may be to increase his speed, but running more slowly will still be an important part of his training; he cannot run fast all the time. In reality, your techniques will be a never-ending change from hardness to softness and back again while moving through the various stages of a technique. To the self your *aiki* should feel soft, while to your partner it should feel as hard as nails, but in a polite kind of way. To

an onlooker, it may look as though *uke* took a dive. Just as there is no 'hard' or 'soft' water, so there are no hard or soft styles or techniques. In fact, the two are inseparable; heavy and light waves flow into each other.

People often talk of hard or soft styles or hard or soft training. The usual context for this type of discussion is some schools claiming that they train harder than others, and that their method is better. The hard think the soft are fairies; the soft think the hard are gorillas. If all you do is soft Aikido, then you probably will be an *aiki* fairy; if all you do is brutish Aikido, then you will indeed be a gorilla. It is as simple as that. As usual, common sense lies in compromise. It is wise to practise both extremes and exist somewhere in the middle. If you must have only one aim, be neither hard nor soft, just be vigorous. Quite often, both the so-called hard or soft schools can be just too slow. You should also be flexible in approach: train hard with the strong, vigorously with the fit, and gently with the frail.

Large or Small Circles

Aikido consists of many movements that can be branded as being either large or small circles. Large circles involve large rotations or sweeping movements of the body, arms and legs; small circles are described by smaller, tighter movements. Many equate the smaller movements as focusing only on the wrist but this is a mistake; the smaller movements include the body and the arm, as well as the wrist. Both offer insight and it is a great disadvantage to over-practise one in preference to the other. Indeed, it is possible to put small circles into large movements, mixing large and small together. Further, combining arm and body movements creates spirals.

Distance

Where you are in the moment goes some way towards deciphering the available shape you recognize in *uke*. For example, *kote-gaeshi* is done from an arm's length or so from *uke*; for *shiho-nage*, you move closer; for *irimi-nage*, you traverse behind.

Straight Line or a Circle

Which is faster, an attack in a straight line or one in a circle? To consider this question, first isolate the feet from the equation – do not move. Now, if you thrust with a sword at a target, the hands must cover a distance of, say, 12in (30cm) in a straight line to strike. If you deliver a downblow to that same target from above, the weapon may move through a distance of 3ft (90cm) or more, while the hands still move through about 12in. The point here is that the blow, in travelling further, has gained much more momentum for a similar amount of hand movement. No doubt the

thrust is faster and the downblow more powerful, but with hard training the speed of a downblow improves considerably. As is usual, the faster student is likely to be the one who has trained harder.

Even if the thrust is determined to be better, it must be remembered that in historic European duels, rapier duellists, while boasting of their speed, typically suffered several thrusting 'hits' before being incapacitated. The result of a single heavy sabre blow was far more debilitating.

Pain

Pain is a great principle. Once the technique is on, it should stay on for the whole technique. If the technique is not on, *uke* should stand up. *Nikyo* is one of the most painful Aikido techniques and should be performed quite differently from *ikkyo*. With *ikkyo*, you lead *uke*'s attack down to the floor along his arm. *Nikyo* is similar but a pain factor is added. This time, in

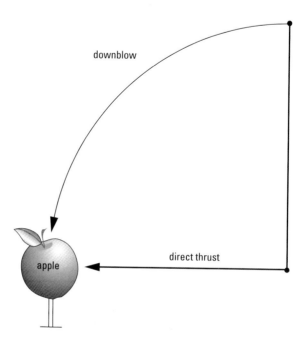

downblow

direct thrust

apple

A direct thrust is quicker, but not as powerful as a downblow.

Weapons teach imperative avoidance.

addition to what you have learned in *ikkyo*, *uke* is led by pain, all the way down. It need not be excruciating, but it has to be 'on', otherwise it is false.

For *nikyo-irimi*, pain is applied in such a way that *uke* opens up for an *irimi* entry. Conversely, for *tenkan*, you apply the pain drawing *uke* forward towards your own centre, then moving to the side, enabling a *tenkan* movement. You should not push the pain towards *uke* for *tenkan* because that would necessitate an *irimi* technique.

Weapons

Teachers can tell students to 'avoid' a thousand times without them ever doing it, yet after only a few lessons training with weapons any student will soon begin to understand. You do need not to be a master swordsman to steal the principles from weapons movement and apply them to Aikido. No one will escape a few raps across the knuckles, and all will become wary of the point. The result is a natural avoiding movement that can easily be adapted to Aikido as *uke* strikes, or takes hold, or does both.

Another interesting way to practise is for *tori* to take a *bokken* when doing *ninin-dori*. All *tori* has to do is avoid slightly and cautiously chop the *ukes* who just walk in. Doing this is great practice for avoidance, for developing *irimi* and *taisabaki* movements, and it also teaches important lessons in distance – even with a *bokken*, you have to be surprisingly close to *uke* to strike.

Practising with a *jo* allows both *tori* and *uke* to make or receive powerful hits fairly safely. You learn not to block, but to deflect or parry, and you need not parry if you have confidence in avoidance. Indeed, you need not even avoid if the combined parry-strike is strong. Also, when thrusting, you do not strike randomly, but you have a defined target. Another way to practise is to have *uke* grab *tori*'s *jo*. *Tori* projects *uke* according to the movements in Aikido, in the spirit of *kokyu-nage*. The simpler the technique the more the student will learn; complicated techniques are less useful. Here, both hands must contain equal energy and must push along the *jo*, in the direction of its strength. If the *jo* bends or breaks, this is considered to be bad technique. It may bend slightly, but a little or not at all is better. Why? You should consider pushing along the *jo* as being equivalent to projecting with *kokyu-nage* using your unbendable arm. Consider bending the *jo* as using your strength. Practice combined with careful thinking will make it clear.

Keep form simple. Learning complicated weapon forms with or without a partner before getting the hang of the basics is the sure road to ruin. What is learned in the beginning sticks like glue, and, if learned wrong, it will stay wrong for a long time. It is very hard to recognize, let alone undo, a bad habit. If you must perform a long-weapon form, think of it as a library of separate techniques, break it down and practise its shorter constituent parts. It is far easier to get a feel of the movement with short-weapon forms. Two or three movements concentrating on one detail should suffice.

One major problem is that many people carry themselves differently when using a weapon. In Aikido, what you do with the *bokken* and *jo* should correspond exactly to what happens in ordinary Aikido practice. If it does not match, then something is wrong, and you will develop contrary bodily movement habits that will serve only to confuse. In this situation, even if you train for fifty years you will never know what you are doing.

Latent Potential

The fact that practitioners of other arts sometimes have *aiki*, yet do not know they have it, is quite interesting. In return, some *aikidoka* have attributes that are found in other arts such as Taichichuan, Pakua, Wing Chun or Jujutsu. While the external forms obviously differ, these arts do share some similar internalized principles. Therefore, training in another art can enable the discerning *aikidoka* to become more aware of what they might already know without knowing. Of course, in the beginning, the arts will seem quite separate, and many may like to keep it that way. After time, forced separateness may deem them incompatible, but reasoned thinking will allow an exchange of similarities, or principles, to take place in the direction of the favoured art. Accordingly, practitioners will then have an idea of how to recognize, describe and pass on such principles that were hitherto apparent, yet unrealized. The most important thing to remember is that, in borrowing, the student takes the principle but not necessarily the form.

Going Too Far

Bruce Lee claimed to teach only the essence of Wing Chun, disregarding less essential elements that he deemed to be unimportant. However, were his students not rather curious to know what he had discarded? After all, it was his skill in Wing Chun that made him famous. It is up to the teacher to teach the totality of the art and it is up to the student to decide whether he likes it or not – this decision is more often than not based on what he can physically do. That student, on becoming a teacher, has the same responsibility to teach the totality. That means, for example, that a student who does Karate and cannot do high kicks should not become a teacher.

A student may abandon a principle if he cannot physically do it, but a teacher has to teach the principles. A student can get away with saying, 'I do not believe in high kicks,' but a teacher of that art has to be able to do them, and to do them well. Furthermore, a teacher has to be able to disprove the 'I do not believe in high kicks' argument and show that they can be done, that the said principle can be shown, and with power and grace. There are many people out there who can do excellent high kicks. Do not blame the technique; the answer lies closer to home – just admit that you cannot do it.

13 Attack

The object of war is not to die for your country but to make the other bastard die for his. *George Patton*

Attacks must be committed since *tori* needs realistic energy against which to train. One school of thought insists that attacks be so committed that *uke* over-extends, almost falling over of his own accord. Others say that *uke* should resist to the utmost and not over-extend at all. Not surprisingly, it is best for *tori* to practise at both extremes to get a feeling for the range of possibilities available. It is also good for *uke* to attack in varying degrees so as to learn how it feels to be off-balance, or not. Certainly, to stick to just one method is not useful. A natural aim is to be realistic.

Uke remains aware and responsive throughout the technique.

The Living *Uke*

Uke is alive and remains conscious throughout the technique so needs to act alive and be responsive. *Uke* should not play dead but provide *tori* with ceaseless responsive pressure. One method to develop this responsiveness is for *uke* constantly to try to stand up with gentle pressure. Accordingly, whenever a gap allowing him to do so appears, *uke* stands up; if *tori* spots it in time, he deals with it as necessary. This should not be a struggle, rather it is a case of *uke* letting *tori* know that a large gap exists.

In contrast, it is not sensible for *uke* to fight against an armlock; someone who resists an armlock is transmitting the unspoken message, 'Please break my arm!' Developing a responsive body is in agreement with developing good *aiki*.

Grabbing Attacks

It is often stated that the striking attacks of Aikido reflect Japan's sword tradition. In the same way, the hand- and cloth-grabbing attacks also reflect tradition since the *keikogi*, or training suit, is in the style of traditional Japanese dress – there is no neck-tie pull, for example. It is natural to reason then that, as Aikido developed alongside Kendo and Judo in modern times, so Aikido defences were designed based on the threat paradigm of the times, namely, sweeping sword cuts or thrusts, and cloth- or arm-grabbing. With that in mind, it makes sense to try Aikido against fast Kendo attacks and strong Judo grasps.

Unlike many other arts, Aikido attacks are done on both left and right sides and from both *ai-hanmi* and *gyakyu-hanmi*. Initially confusing, this method leads to advanced co-ordination. There are many different grabbing attacks but what is important is to realize the similarities in movements between them. While they look different, they often feel almost exactly the same. For example, basic *ai-hanmi katate-dori* techniques unfold in almost exactly the same way as *ai-hanmi shomen-uchi* ones – they are linked in principle. The same relationship exists between *gyaku-hanmi katate-dori* and *yokomen-uchi* techniques. Even the attacks are similar. In *shomen-uchi*, *uke* attacks to the front; in *yokomen uchi*, *uke* attacks slightly to the side. Correspondingly, in *ai-hanmi katate-dori*, *uke* is in front of *tori*; in *gyaku-hanmi katate-dori*, *uke* is slightly to the side. What this means is that variations in technique from grabbing attacks can often be applied to striking attacks. *Ryote-dori* techniques commonly unfold in the same way as *gyaku-hanmi* ones; *ushiro-ryote-dori* techniques unfold like *ai-hanmi* ones. Most Aikikai-based schools start *morote-dori* attacks from *gyaku-hanmi* so, for the inquisitive, it is worth taking a look at *ai-hanmi* variations.

There are many more grabbing attacks and much of the movement within each corresponds to the basic *ai-hanmi/gyaku-hanmi katate-dori* distinctions; the only real differences are found in the initial movements. *Ushiro* attacks commonly start from a static position but it is better in training to have *uke* walk around to the rear and for *tori* to begin the technique a little early. Later, you turn your back slightly, offering both hands to lure *uke*. Later still, after the lure, you use body movement, transferring your momentum to send *uke* around increasingly faster to the rear. *Kata-dori* attacks, front or rear, are ideal for practising body movement – try to use your body as much as possible when drawing *uke* around, without disengaging *uke*'s grip until the last moment.

With solid training, one important principle is that the closer to *tori*'s hand *uke* grabs, the harder it is for *tori* to make

A right *shomen-uchi* begins its power stroke as the right foot passes the left.

technique. The lowest point on the arm to grab is where the arm and hand meet, at the wrist joint. Any lower and *uke* is beginning to make his own technique on *tori*'s hand.

Striking Attacks

Making a Striking Attack

The main striking attacks in Aikido are *shomen-uchi*, *yokomen-uchi* and *tsuki*. Some schools also add *gyaku yokomen-uchi* and *uraken*. Occasionally, there is an uppercut.

In more modern terms, *shomen-uchi* reflects a simple downblow, *yokomen-uchi* a roundhouse blow. One method to practise developing heavy striking power is to hit the mat hard when break-falling. Interestingly, in dealing with these striking attacks, *tori* often responds in like manner, meeting *shomen-uchi* with *shomen-uchi*, and so on.

Uke should make a solid, calculated, dynamic attack. When raising the arm for a one-step *shomen-uchi*, the body should move forwards slightly as the arm raises but the rear foot must not yet pass the front. The rear foot only passes once the strike is on its way down, otherwise the closing distance will leave a large inviting gap for *tori* to take advantage of with an easy *jodan-tsuki* or *shomen-ate*. It is also good practice for *uke* to hesitate, trying to confuse *tori*. Alternatively, *uke* can walk around a little, exhibiting different footwork before initiating the attack. For *yokomen-uchi* it is best to raise the striking arm up as in *shomen-uchi* – in front of the head. Swinging it rearwards often results in too much telegraphing and, worse, your own body might even follow it by winding back with the movement.

For *tsuki* attacks, avoid the Karate-style retracting fist; in Aikido it is best to keep both hands forwards to maintain balance, even when punching. Furthermore, the Aikido punch is performed more like a thrust, often done vertically with the thumb uppermost. It is almost as if punching with a knife, using the upper two knuckles of the fist, and with the body weight behind it, rather than being like a boxing jab or Karate twisting punch. Although slower, it will have a very forceful effect if striking home.

Rare in the traditional styles is *shomen-ate*, an open-palm strike upwards to the chin. Rather than being a hand strike, with the body behind it, it necessarily becomes a powerful push, and it is difficult to see it coming as it emerges from below.

Of course, it is up to each student to vary his training according to taste, and, although they are rare in Aikido, it certainly makes sense to develop a few strong, low kicks in solo practice. Teachers should encourage this.

Dealing with Striking Attacks

Typically, against a *shomen-uchi* attack, *tori*

will make a *shomen-uchi* movement; against a *yokomen-uchi* attack, *tori* will make a *yokomen-uchi* movement. Making the same type of movement makes it easier for *tori* to learn to harmonize with *uke*. Once harmony is present after sustained practice, *tori* can, if desired, deal with a *yokomen-uchi* by using *shomen-uchi* movements, and vice versa.

After further practice, *tori* can begin to change the time, starting either earlier or later than the incoming attack. For example, if *uke*'s raising and descending blow is imagined to comprise 360 degrees of movement, by starting 180 degrees late *tori* can cut up strongly as *uke* cuts down, hitting his arm and deflecting it. Against a right-handed *yokomen-uchi* attack, a left-handed *gyaku-yokomen-uchi* movement helps deflect, and a right-handed *shomen-uchi* to *uke*'s arm ought to knock it down, disable it, and allow *tori* to get through to *uke*'s rear.

Innumerable combinations can be mixed together to make interesting practice.

Faster than a Flying Fist

Despite being a common sight in Aikido, 'catching a flying fist' is almost impossible in reality. Aikido movement originates from the centre of the body and a moving body cannot easily match the speed of the fist of someone adept at a hand art, whose training initiates movement in the hand. *Judoka* control the body and move out towards the arm; Judo is a body art. In Aikido, the practitioner should control the mind of the opponent first, and then his body; distracting the opponent's attention takes the mind, providing the opportunity to control the head, body, arm or hand, or whatever becomes available in the moment.

In dealing with a *tsuki* attack it is not really practical just to catch it and move into, say, *ikkyo*. Many of the standard *tsuki kihon-waza* need considerable modification to be of any real practical use. If your intention is to take hold of the arm – and it must be if many Aikido techniques are to be performed – you can first try to distract by flicking fingers at eyes, or by feigning a kick to the groin. In feigning an attack, *tori* is searching for a response from *uke*. If *uke* raises his arms up in protection, *tori* might be able to take hold and perform *ikkyo*. If *uke* does not raise the arms up in self-protection, *tori* should hit him again!

Second, rather than grabbing the arm, it helps to hook it first with the lower fingers; grabbing it reduces your own options. With a loose grip, you are still somewhat free to change.

Third, keep in mind possible combinations – a switch to *waki-gatame*, or *ude-garami* may be possible. If it is *ikkyo* that is to be the result, then momentarily applying a *waki-gatame*-style movement may disorient him enough to return safely to *ikkyo*.

Another method is to forget *ikkyo* temporarily, move in for *irimi-nage*, and, when throwing him down at the floor, take the nearest arm for *ikkyo*, if it is *ikkyo* that must be done. The root of the problem of techniques such as *tsuki ikkyo* is that people imagine the *tsuki* to be a jab, rather than a thrust with the body weight behind it. The jab is from an art that is of the hand-first type, the thrust from a body-first type. The jab is faster and standard Aikido often cannot cope with it; *aikidoka* need to accept that fact and concentrate more on avoidance. In dealing with a hand-art player, *aikidoka* need to use their skill to survive temporarily playing them at their own game, then draw them into their own body-art environment where, hopefully, the hand-art player lacks skill.

Initiating the Attack

Facing *uke* in posture is confrontational and could be said to be provoking attack. Offering the wrist is a lure, and it could be said that *tori* is inviting the attack. Feigning attack to create a response to use in your technique is initiating an attack. *Tori* can also initiate the attack by just hitting *uke*, then deal with *uke*'s response. In fact, in certain schools, *tori* initiates grabbing techniques with a *shomen-uchi*, which *uke* deflects down, then moving to the side to take hold as in *kata-dori* or *morote-dori*. In initiating the attack, you have anticipated trouble and are acting accordingly. If you hit *uke*, then *uke* is hit; if *uke* responds, then *aiki* can develop.

In a sense, initiating an attack is a kind of lure in Aikido that allows *tori* to take control of the time. If the object is to grasp *uke*'s arm, then you could feign to *uke* in order to make him raise his arm to a position where it could be grabbed. In a steal from Jujutsu, you could create a hip throw in the moment. Rather than spotting a shape and taking advantage, *tori* lures or leads *uke*, creates the desired shape and takes advantage as it is being created. For example, if *uke* is in right posture, *tori* feigns a kick at *uke*'s front knee with the instep of his right foot. As *uke* retreats his leg in avoidance, *tori* advances and moves forward in harmony stepping in with the right foot and entering for, say, *koshi-nage*. If *tori* can move in at exactly the same time that *uke* retreats his leg then *tori* will be in position for the throw at the moment the shape for it is created. This is not about timing or fast reflexes, but about control and harmony.

Atemi

It is often said that Aikido is 90 per cent *atemi*. While something of an enigma, if *atemi* is co-ordinated and well focused

Tori attacks.

Uke meets the attack.

Uke delivers first *atemi* to eyes with the left hand.

Uke delivers second *atemi* to eyes with the right hand.

within *aiki* movement, then it certainly helps make the technique work. Note that *atemi* here usually refers to strikes performed by *tori* in the midst of technique. The key in delivering *atemi* is in not interrupting the flow of the technique, thereby disturbing the *aiki*. Rather, it ought to contribute to the *aiki* flow. This is a very important point that is often completely ignored.

While the most obvious form of *atemi* is a direct punch or kick to a vulnerable point, there are more dangerous forms of *atemi*:

- jabbing at the eyes with the fingers;
- stroking the back of the hand across the eyes using the fingernails;
- hitting the side of the neck or throat with the inner or outer forearms;
- hitting *uke*'s arms with the forearms;
- clapping a hand over the ear;
- using a back-fist to the lower ribs or hammer-fist to the kidneys;
- delivering an upper back-fist or kick to the groin; or
- head-butting *uke* when taking control as in *sankyo* or moving in close for *koshi-nage*.

When close in, a knee to the groin or inner/outer thigh area will temporarily incapacitate *uke*. A man has a natural instinct to protect the groin, so consider hitting or kicking the bladder instead; it is very effective and totally unexpected. An open hand is far more powerful than a fist for the average person, especially for those who do not train to punch. Indeed, boxers are commonly known to break their own fists in pub brawls, when their ego gets the better of them. Alternatively, use a fist for striking soft areas, and an open palm-heel for the hard. Remember, it is important to aim every strike.

In order to solve the enigma, to acquire the idea of what real *atemi* in Aikido is, you need to practise constantly with the *bokken*. The *shomen* and *yokomen* striking movements can become principles in themselves that can be incorporated into your techniques, whether you use them as strikes or not. In empty-hand techniques, the up-and-down movements of *shomen-uchi* can be performed as parry, deflection, hit or cut. They can be delivered gently, or painfully. In addition, even when moving into the midst of technique, those same principles used within the up-and-down movements can be applied again in redirecting *uke* to the mat.

Finally, the idea of contact can be thought of as *atemi* in the sense that, if *uke* makes contact with *tori*'s centre, then that in itself constitutes an attack; this implies that, if *tori* makes contact with *uke*'s centre, *tori* is indeed hitting *uke*. Thus, contact is subsequently maintained for the remaining 90 per cent of the technique.

Half-a-Hand and Full Hand

It is traditionally implied that half-a-hand hits heavily enough to knock out, while the full hand kills. For more realistic training in Aikido it is useful to take this principle and tame it. For Aikido, half-a-hand can be taken to be a strike within the movement that may clonk the head, slap the face, touch the eyeball, or penetrate the body enough that it actually jolts *uke* slightly, for real, not play, and that an onlooker would 'feel' it. From *uke*'s point of view there is no lasting effect other than a slight toughening up over time.

In contrast, the full hand hits much harder – a real blow that is enough to incapacitate *uke*, making him almost fall into the technique. However, this kind of full hand does not mean hitting with full force, as hard as you can hit. There is still

One-third up from the wrist.

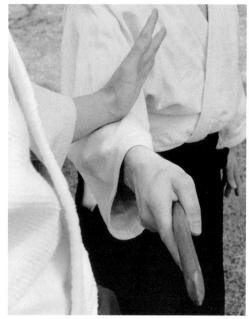

One-third down from the elbow.

One-third down from the shoulder.

control. From time to time, one needs to negotiate with *uke* and incorporate such half-hand strikes into the techniques properly to appreciate the power of Aikido. Obviously, the full hand is only for life-threatening self-defence (*see* Appendix III).

To develop the half hand, practise hitting *uke* in various places using different strikes, such as a gentle punch, palm heel, back-fist, finger jab, shin kick, and so on. Such strikes should give *uke* a slight jolt, being either slow and heavy, or light and fast, but not too uncomfortable. To develop the full hand, first hit the mat hard and heavy during *ukemi*, or just whack the forearm into the mat, then direct it at *uke* and aim to hit with full force, but at the last moment stop short.

Striking Point

When *tori* contacts *uke*'s arm it should be in the form of an Aikido-based movement such as *yokomen-uchi* or *shomen-uchi*. This movement can be light or heavy in feeling, and a parry, hit or cut in form; when striking, it is vital to aim. For many Aikido techniques it is useful to aim to hit *uke*'s arm heavily, approximately one-third of the way down from the elbow, or sometimes one-third of the way down from the shoulder. Here, momentum is transferred to *uke*'s arm with the prerequisite amount of pain. If the arm is hit any lower, it will probably be dashed away.

Another point to aim for is approximately one-third of the way up from *uke*'s wrist. This lighter target needs a more jabby, lighter hit. When hitting heavily, *tori* uses a point about one-third of the way along his own forearm from the wrist, for lighter hits, closer to, or using, the *tegatana* is fine. Both of these types of hit can be done from inside or outside of *uke*'s arms and this same feeling of striking can be used on other, more vulnerable areas of *uke*'s anatomy to great effect.

14 Techniques

I have never let my schooling interfere with my education.
Mark Twain

With good posture and awareness it is difficult for *uke* to find an opening for attack. This is particularly obvious when practising with a *bokken* or *jo*, which you have to lower or retract to the side slightly to let *uke* in. Moreover, even while the technique progresses, *uke* is still supposed to attack, poking at any *suki* that appear in *tori*'s technique. *Uke*, too, responds in such a way as to reduce the *suki* available to *tori*. In fact, it is said that, once all the *suki* for *atemi* are closed, all that is left is Aikido technique.

Discerning Differences

Rather than 'techniques', the concept of 'shapes' is preferable – an attempt to escape from the form. However, that is not to suggest that form should be avoided; for beginners it is essential. The form is a necessary introduction to any martial art, and this is certainly the case in Aikido. With a little experience under your belt, good basics, good *ukemi*, a few gradings, and a good amount of *kokyu-nage*, you will have become quite familiar with the basic patterns of Aikido. The emphasis here is on 'patterns'. Now, it will become helpful to regard the techniques as shapes – *ikkyo* shape, *nikyo* shape or *kaiten-nage* shape. This approach will help the student to come to terms with the vast number of variations that exist.

Aikidoka, perhaps more than most other martial artists, often hold courses where a mixture of styles meet. Often, they pay friendly visits to other *dojos*. It is while participating in these kinds of activities that confusion can set in for the unwary. What results is a classification of styles, or *dojos* – we do it this way, they do it that way, another *dojo* does it another way – apparently creating different sets of what is essentially the same knowledge. The key to learning Aikido is to look for the commonalities, not the differences, since it is only in the common principles that solid foundations lie.

At first, common principles are not always obvious to the uninitiated; a discerning eye is needed. Furthermore, even among the differences you may find other hidden principles just waiting to be grasped. For example, a difference that you discern at another school might be a very good principle that your own school lacks. It is also the case that some of these differences may be bad, although the problem may lie in your own method, not in theirs. Honest retrospection is the key through which the answers will emerge.

There are many *ikkyo* shapes. If you can make a particular *ikkyo* shape work, it makes sense to adopt it in your repertoire. If you cannot make it work, but others can, then the problem obviously lies with you. Suspect the technique last. More often than not, the differences between variations seem to be simply mechanical – a different foot is forward or a different entry is used. However, with a simply mechanistic view of the techniques, there would be no end to the number of variations to remember. Indeed, this is the way many people train. That different entry is not a mechanical difference but represents a new principle that could be applied elsewhere, in other 'shapes'. By thinking about it and trying to make that new entry fit into another 'shape', the student will automatically assign it as a useful principle. You need not remember that particular *ikkyo* variation; just remember the new principle

so that it helps to create your own new personal variations. Of course, they will not really be new, nor your own, as others have already discovered them a thousand times before, but there is nothing better than to discover, to feel in control of your learning experience, and not be completely dependent upon a teacher.

This is where the voyage of discovery really begins and it may explain what is meant by the assertion 'the *Shodan* is just a beginner'. The *Shodan* has the tools and should have all the pieces, so must now set to work putting them together and figuring

Ikkyo irimi shape.

Ikkyo irimi midway.

Start palm-up, try *ikkyo*.

Start thumb-up, try *ikkyo*.

Start palm-down, try *ikkyo*.

Start thumb-down, try *ikkyo*.

out what it all means. However, there is no need to wait until *Shodan* to begin. When meeting in vigorous practice you have little time to think: you meet *uke*, recognize a shape such as *ikkyo* or *kaiten-nage*, and take it. One way to practise this is for *uke* and *tori* to run and clash into each other, gently-ish. At the moment of random clash, both pause, *tori* looks at *uke* and examines the situation, trying to recognize a shape. Once *tori* recognizes something, it is used and technique materializes.

After you have a grasp of what principles are and can apply them to your own *aiki*, then, and only then, will you be able to look at what others are doing and say with certainty, 'That is correct,' or, 'That is wrong.' In the long run, it will help distinguish sound technique from bad variation. People often criticize good form. It may not be good form in a certain school, but it is good form nevertheless, which indicates that they do not know. It is perhaps natural that, when visiting other schools, the tradition in martial arts is to do it their way; the purpose in visiting another school is to learn new ways, not to show your own. Certainly, when visiting other schools, wise students look for new principles, not new form.

Technical Tips

The following are not descriptions of how to do the techniques; the assumption is that the student already knows the basic 'shapes'. Below are added tips on how to do those techniques with different flavours. All descriptions are from the point of view of *tori* in right posture, unless otherwise stated.

Ikkyo

Ikkyo is useful as it is the simplest of the immobilization techniques in the sense that *tori* grabs *uke*'s arm and presses *uke* down to the floor. The tricky part is getting your co-ordination right while being in the right place at the right time. Imagine the moment when *uke* takes *tori*'s arm. In terms of co-ordination, the key is for *tori* first to determine how *uke* grabs.

There are four main arm positions: palm-up, thumb-up, palm-down and thumb-down. It would certainly be wise to practise being grabbed from all four positions as in each case the technique will start, and unfold, differently. Also, *tori* could offer palm-up (or whatever), yet turn the arm to one of the remaining three positions just as *uke* takes hold. It is perhaps natural that one of the biggest problems beginners have is failing to determine the initial position of the teacher's wrist/arm and how it changes, and this is true for all other hand-grabbing attacks. In terms of space, when attacked *tori* needs to adjust his position rearwards slightly, or more, so that *uke* can grab either strongly, lightly or barely at all. Obviously, the further back you go, the weaker *uke*'s grab will be and the easier it will be for *tori* to start.

It is also useful to avoid moving slightly to the left, or to the right while moving back, both of which modify the technique differently. For an *ai-hanmi katate-dori* attack, avoiding to the rear left will leave you on the outside of *uke*'s arms; avoiding to the rear right will take you to the inside; avoiding straight back will leave you central. All are viable and can be further modified by time – the feeling of entering early, at the same time, or late. *Tori* can begin technique at different times yet still maintain a sense of harmony with *uke*.

One powerful variation is for *tori* not to grasp *uke*'s elbow at all, but instead to place his arm on it palm-downwards, and

Non-standard *nikyo* release.

LEFT: Standard *nikyo* shape.

then to rotate it palm-up while thrusting the arm forwards slightly. This will roll *uke*'s arm over sending him to the ground very quickly indeed; be careful not to do it too hard, as it is his turn next!

One uncommon, but very powerful, variation of *ikkyo* is for tori to catch *uke*'s arm from underneath, just above *uke*'s elbow with the palm-up. This grip sometimes happens naturally, such as when *uke* misbehaves, bending his elbow downwards to resist *ikkyo*. This allows *tori* the option of a strong jerk to disorient *uke*, after which the opportunity to re-enter *ikkyo* might be created; otherwise, a follow-up technique, such as *irimi-nage*, could be attempted.

Other good variations include entering your hips under *uke*'s arm and projecting, tripping by blocking *uke*'s closest leg with your own, or modifying using *koshi-nage*.

All of the above ideas can be called principles and, with a little thought, can be applied in many other techniques.

Nikyo
Nikyo can be done in much the same way as *ikkyo*. When holding *uke* in *nikyo*, make sure that his hand and thumb are grasped firmly, and that you move from your own centre to apply the technique. The more *uke*'s elbow bends towards 90 degrees, the easier it is to apply pain to the wrist. It is also important for *tori* to show control – *tori*'s slight movement applies technique that provokes a much larger movement in *uke*.

There are several common variations of holding. In *nikyo*, some wring the wrist and hand as if squeezing water out of a wet flannel. Some concentrate on the up-and-down motion of *uke*'s hand and cut down

Sankyo grip.

uke's centre through the pain in the hand; some think of *nikyo* as a kind of reverse *sankyo*, screwing the hand in towards *uke*'s face, making him scurry around to the rear; some take their free left hand over *uke*'s arm so completely that their own elbow passes that of *uke*; some take it further over and under, latching on to their own right hand for extra leverage; some take the free left arm under *uke*'s arm and push against *uke*'s elbow from the inside; some modify the latter variation by pushing their hand under *uke*'s arm and up, taking *uke*'s hand into an even more powerful wristlock; some take *uke*'s wrist and press it into their chest then push forwards to make technique; some even put *uke*'s wrist on their forehead and make a small nod or bow to apply pain; some press *uke*'s wrist and elbow together.

Nikyo can also be combined with *koshi-nage*. It can be done in much the same way as *ikkyo koshi-nage* projection, or the pain can be used to push *uke*'s elbow up high like *sankyo*, thereby drawing *uke* closer, then throwing straight down with *koshi-nage*.

No matter what *nikyo* variant *tori* does, however, from *uke*'s point of view it ought to be pretty much the same kind of pain. An important point to note is that, when applying the wristlock, you can either push *uke* away slightly, or draw him nearer. Obviously, he should be pushed away for an *irimi* entrance, and drawn nearer for *tenkan*. Confusing the two leads to an untidy technique.

Sankyo

Sankyo is a reversal of the *nikyo* wrist position. While it is standard to take *uke* down while walking backwards, one simple and effective variation is to perform a standard *ikkyo* while grabbing the fingers, instead of the wrist, to make a *sankyo* bowed-arm shape. Finish by increasing the pressure of the twist while still behind *uke*'s arm in the apparent *ikkyo*-like position. Another similar variation is to take *uke* down as before but then switch hands, remaining behind the bowed arm with your own hands reversed, again finishing by increasing the pressure.

Sankyo is a powerful technique and it is easy for *tori* to get used to the idea of leading *uke* around by the point of his elbow. The pain is in the wrist but the secret lies in the elbow. This kind of idea is useful in other techniques, especially *yonkyo*. Interestingly, you can drop *uke*'s elbow by pointing it at the floor to the front or rear; pointing it to the front results in an ordinary finish; pointing it to the rear means that *uke* may be flipped over or thrown down like a sack of potatoes.

Nikyo can be done in a similar manner, becoming a kind of *kote-gaeshi* variant, as can *ikkyo*, which then turns into *ude garami-nage*.

Yonkyo

Yonkyo is one of the most difficult techniques. In essence, the general movement is much the same as *sankyo*, but inflicting pain on *uke*'s inner wrist is the main problem; on some people it is easy, while on others it is nigh-on impossible. In order to learn it better it is best to isolate the *yonkyo* grip from the rest of the technique. Simply grab your partner's palm-up wrist and practise pressing down on it with the inner knuckle of the forefinger. The weakest points – which are therefore target points – are the corners of the inner wrist, although it is sometimes done on the outside corners on the back of the wrist. The closer to the hand, the easier it is to generate the pain. Just pressing is not enough. It should feel as though you are collecting a bunch of nerves in the knuckle and then

Yonkyo grip.

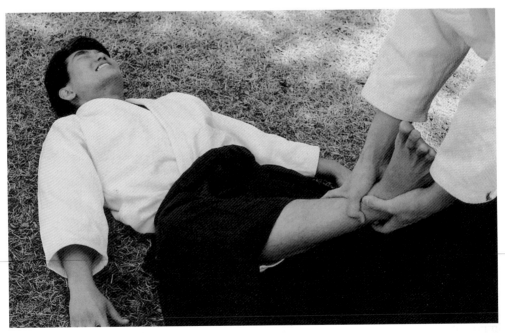

Yonkyo grip on the inner ankle.

Gokyo grip.

manipulating them slightly over a bone, then pressing. If it seems like a certain person is immune, hold a pen or stick in the palm and press the flat side (not the point) of it into their wrist like *yonkyo*. This also works quite well on the bony back of the hand and ought at least to show that *yonkyo* is possible on most people.

Yonkyo is a useful holding grip in many techniques. In *ikkyo*, holding with a *yonkyo* grip in both hands prevents you from using too much strength, and might even cause a little *yonkyo* pain in the wrist if performed well. When performing *nikyo* and *sankyo* it is similarly possible to include a modicum of *yonkyo* pain at the same time as part of the technique. In *shiho-nage*, applying *yonkyo* pressure to *uke*'s wrist can sometimes help; however, if it is too painful, *shiho-nage* itself might become impossible as *uke* collapses in a heap. Holding a *bokken* or *jo* using a *yonkyo* grip

gives a clue to direction in movement. Of course, it follows that, in applying *yonkyo* more universally, your own *yonkyo* power will improve.

Gokyo

Gokyo is the same as *ikkyo*, but with the wrist-grabbing hand reversed. It is often taught as a response to a knife attack, as gripping in this way ensures the blade is a little further from your own wrist. Accordingly, it is most often performed against knife attacks but it deserves more favour than that. From the outside of *uke*'s arms, *ikkyo* is the usual response, but *gokyo* is also possible. From the inside, especially from *yokomen-uchi*, while *ikkyo* is done without question in daily practice, logic dictates that *gokyo* would be far more suitable, since it is so easy to catch *uke*'s wrist with *gokyo* to strongly take control.

Waki-gatame.

With ordinary *ikkyo*, it is not possible easily to lift *uke*'s hand; instead, you have to wait for *uke* to do so of his own accord, then take advantage. Simply, if *gokyo* is good enough for knife defences, it ought to be good enough for empty-hand attacks too. Indeed, on grabbing *uke*'s (right) wrist from the inside, by necessity, *tori*'s (right) hand is palm-down. By turning the body (to the right) and twisting his own arm to a palm-up position, *tori* can generate a lot of power, should that be required. Accordingly, it makes sense to practise *gokyo* from *katate-dori* or *ryote-dori* attacks as well. When practising *gokyo* from *sode-dori* or *mune-dori* attacks, it is essential to break the cloth grip first. If *uke* offers a resisting straight arm, *gokyo* can work as an armlock takedown. To enter, *tori* reverse twists *uke*'s arm contrary to the *ikkyo* roll, twisting wrist and elbow in reverse as though wringing a towel. At this time, it is useful to push along *uke*'s arm to press his

shoulder down to the floor. If done this way, *gokyo* becomes related to *ude-gatame*, and change is possible to *waki-gatame* if necessary.

Rokkyo

Rokkyo, otherwise known as *waki-gatame* (not to be confused with *ude-gatame*), is the technique that can be used when all other immobilizations fail. With *uke*'s arm held locked out against your chest in a little-finger-up shape, it is quite similar to *nikyo*. Indeed, should *uke* succeed in struggling to bend the arm at the elbow, *nikyo* is the result, yet a side elbow lock can be incorporated at the same time, if desired. Should *uke* force his arm straight from *nikyo*, then *rokkyo* is the result – they are perfect cousins.

This technique needs to be practised against every form of attack. The main problem with it is that it is an armlock and, as such, some schools disregard it,

Ude-gatame.

considering armlocks to be anti-Aikido. Sometimes, philosophy gains over common sense.

Ude-Gatame

Ude-gatame, sometimes called *ude-hishige*, differs from *waki-gatame* in that *uke*'s palm faces upwards and, as a result, the elbow is pressed straight down. Rather crude when compared to *waki-gatame*, it is none the less quite effective. It forms the same kind of elbow pressure that is used when projecting in *mae-otoshi* or *juji-nage* and can also be used within other techniques to send *uke* flying down towards the *tatami* for an *ikkyo* immobilization.

Irimi-Nage

Irimi-nage is one of the most basic of Aikido throws and, in a sense, mirrors *kaiten-nage* in shape – if *uke* refuses to get up or be thrown back, you can switch to *kaiten-nage*, and vice-versa. It is, perhaps,

Irimi-nage.

Irimi-nage variation.

one of the easiest techniques to come to terms with and the first throw that needs to be mastered. One interesting observation is that, while many schools practise *irimi* and *tenkan* variants for every technique four times before changing roles, they almost always do four *tenkan* versions of *irimi-nage*, ignoring the *irimi*. However, the *irimi-nage irimi* version (without the initial *tenkan* movement) is of great practical importance, especially in terms of self-defence and it makes no sense to ignore it.

Standard technique is to throw gently along the spine. The most common variation is to displace *uke*'s hips to the right with your own while taking *uke*'s head slightly to the left. Sometimes frowned upon as being un-*aiki*, because it is uncomfortable for *uke* to break-fall, this is a very practical variation. To be fair, you should only practise the same variation as your partner. Other variations include throwing *uke* over your hips to the front or rear, throwing *uke* with the hand on the chin or side of the neck, throwing *uke* by feigning a strike to the face, which *uke* avoids by break-falling, and throwing *uke* by actually striking – gently, of course – the side of the neck.

The highest skill in throwing with *irimi-nage* is derived from throwing your opponent up, not down. What goes up comes down naturally. Here it has become more like *tenchi-nage*, and this is a good example of the way some techniques can merge into each other.

Shiho-Nage
Shiho-nage, almost impossible to do, is the most classic Aikido technique, with a vast number of variations. (This is surely a reflection of Aikido students' struggles to come to terms with it.) Even though you are highly unlikely to beat off five demented muggers with it, practising *shiho-nage* offers many valuable lessons in feeling

Shiho-nage tenkan.

Shiho-nage tenkan – tori's eye view.

and movement. For example, it is most likely to be through this technique that you first begin to realize the importance of contact and centre.

For an effective *shiho-nage*, the student must first come to terms with what is variously referred to as *mae-otoshi, jujigatame-nage, ude hishigi-nage* or *ude kime-nage*. This technique (called here *ude kime-nage*) is similar to the beginning of *shiho-nage* but instead *tori* extends *uke*'s arm out in a twisted semi-armlock and projects *uke* away. There are many soft and fluffy versions of *shiho-nage*, but the key to a truly powerful *shiho-nage* lies in having a powerful *ude kime-nage*. The way the practitioner performs *ude kime-nage* should determine

the entrance for *shiho-nage*; if you can hold *uke* in the junction position just before the *ude kime-nage* throw, then you can convert it to *shiho-nage* without much ado. Failing to unify such common principles indicates that the student does not understand.

Kote-Gaeshi

Kote-gaeshi is probably one of the most practical Aikido techniques. In shape, it is opposite to *nikyo* or *sankyo*, and similar to *shiho-nage*. *Kote-gaeshi* is one of the furthest Aikido techniques – 'furthest' in the sense of distance from *uke* when throwing. The key to getting *kote-gaeshi* correct is to press *uke*'s wrist in line with *uke*'s fingers, towards an imaginary point just outside

Kote-gaeshi.

his elbow, yet with the feeling of screwing inwards towards his centre along his forearm. Twisting it outwards any more is going to hurt; it might make it work, but does not help in learning Aikido. Pressing towards the elbow allows you to maintain the feeling that you are contacting and disturbing *uke*'s centre. *Uke* can fall back, or be led over his own wrist forwards. Dropping your body weight adds a little momentum to the occasion. Further, rather than simply returning *uke*'s hand towards *uke*'s body, you should press or curl the wrist seemingly on the spot, thereby drawing *uke* forwards towards and over his own wrist.

Kote-gaeshi is very powerful and, after *uke*'s balance is disturbed, many other techniques are possible in combination. If combining *kote-gaeshi* with another technique such as *shomen-ate* or *irimi-nage* it is necessary to modify the *kote-gaeshi* grip slightly to get a better one-hand hold. To do this, allow the gripping left hand to slip slightly in the direction of the applied pressure until your thumb just sneaks around

to the back of *uke*'s hand, all the while maintaining control of *uke*'s thumb. A *yonkyo*-type pressure can also be applied to *uke*'s knuckles.

It is a common mistake in *kote-gaeshi* for the fingers of *tori*'s (left) lower hand to extend on to *uke*'s wrist, thereby effectively blocking the application of *tori*'s own technique. The lower hand should hold *uke*'s hand, not his wrist.

Kaiten-Nage
Kaiten-nage is almost ignored in some Aikido styles, which is strange considering it is such a great complement to *irimi-nage* or *tenchi-nage*. Once you are in position to throw, the most common method is to push *uke*'s arm across his back. What is often missed is pressing down the head firmly using the arch of the extended hand. Before placing the hand on the back of the head it is useful to perform a strike, stopping at the last inch for safety, then pressing. A gentle push produces the standard roll. If it is done quickly, *uke* will spin on the spot, landing on his backside. If it is

Kaiten-nage.

done slowly, you can twist *uke* so that he feels like he is twisting out of it, but ends up sitting down, quite open to a range of holds, locks or strangles. If *uke* begins to twist out and stand up, you can let the neck hand follow through, quickly grasp his opposite collar and strangle, with *uke* in a leant-back standing position, by maintaining hold of the throwing arm in a straight armlock. Alternatively, as *uke* begins to resist the standard technique, *tori* might change to *irimi-nage* or *tenchi-nage*.

Kaiten-nage can also be performed after any of the immobilization techniques. It is also useful as a counter to a rugby-style head-first grabbing attack – move to the rear (left) corner, *taisabaki* slightly, and press the head down as *uke* approaches. If

103

uke does not fly with his own momentum, twist your own body making *taisabaki* in the opposite direction and sit him down backwards.

Tenchi-Nage

Tenchi-nage is sometimes known as the 'zigzag throw', referring to the footwork, or the 'heaven and earth throw', referring to the position of the hands. For *ryote-dori* most people zigzag with their feet, but there appear to be several interesting variations in terms of handwork. In the simplest mechanical version, the hands follow the feet; the left hand goes down as the left foot 'zigs', and the right hand goes up as the right foot 'zags' behind *uke*. In most cases, the top hand actually goes down too, as in *irimi-nage*. Some people, however, insist on keeping it up high and making the throw work more with the body entrance; a little harder, but more enlightening considering the name of the throw. By far the best way is to initiate the lower hand as in *tenkan-ho*, with the upper hand cutting up inside *uke*'s wrist. That initial *tenkan-ho* principle is important here – it contacts *uke*'s centre and off-balances, turns circularly, and can lead him anywhere, no matter how hard he grips. In this sense, this technique can be done in much the same way as *suwari-waza kokyu-ho*.

One interesting variation is to place the upper hand on the near side of *uke*'s neck, pushing up with *tegatana* to throw. To make a stronger throw here, you can also grab the cloth of *uke*'s lower arm, or even contemplate Judo variations of an *O soto-gari* shape. By concentrating on the up-and-down motion of *tenchi-nage*, a variation of it can be done from *ushiro ryote-dori*: putting weight in the left hand, step slightly to the left; at the same time, raise the right hand high; a slight rearward step or shuffle should suffice to throw.

Koshi-Nage

Koshi-nage is the technique that many love to hate, some because they cannot do it, and some because of the heavy break-fall. With a little thought, many techniques in Aikido can be converted to *koshi-nage*. The problem here is that hip throws are rarely practised enough in Aikido. Worse, lots of

Tenchi-nage shape.

Koshi-nage.

Koshi-nage variation.

Shomen-ate.

practice in 180-degree *taisabaki* means that many turn in too far to effect a good throw. The Judo hip throw, *O-goshi*, is qualitatively different from that of Aikido's *koshi-nage*. Nevertheless, practising the Judo type in an *aiki* manner will help your throws enormously. The main difference is that, in Judo, for extra power the practitioners straighten their legs, effectively doing the technique 'on' their opponents, and jacking *uke* up and over.

In Aikido, a committed attack means that you must move out of the way, so the throw is more like tripping the opponent up over your hip. An Aikido-type *O-goshi* grabbing the cloth to throw is a good addition to break-falling exercises after the warm-up and a useful introduction to the many *koshi-nage* variations often performed in unison with projections or powerful armlocks.

Shomen-Ate

Shomen-ate, a strong upwards thrust to *uke*'s chin with the heel of the palm, is a devastating Aikido technique. It is not a

Ikkyo.

Nikyo.

Sankyo.

Yonkyo.

Gokyo.

Waki-gatame.

Variation 1.

Variation 2.

hit; the trick is to thrust directly up, in line with *uke*'s centre. Any deviation from the centre will result in your own hand being automatically deflected left or right. The mild version sees *uke* taking gentle *ushiro ukemi*; the strong version sees *uke*'s feet leave the ground. If *uke* has not already been sent flying, then a follow-up with any number of techniques is in order before *uke* regains balance.

Hold-Downs
Hold-downs at the end of techniques im-mobilize *uke*. *Ikkyo, nikyo, sankyo, yonkyo, gokyo* and *rokkyo* each have their own forms. The standard finish for *kote-gaeshi* is generally the *nikyo* finish but there are sev-eral other variations. *Shiho-nage* is usually a projection but it also has its own hold-down form. *Tenchi-nage* and *irimi-nage* have no hold-down form and instead rely on *zanshin* to control *uke*. It is usual to let

Variation 3.

Variation 4.

Variation 5.

uke roll out of *kaiten-nage*, so this technique has no standard end form. There are many other hold-downs and variations beyond the basic forms and it is wise to learn as many as possible.

Other Techniques

There are several other Aikido techniques such as *ude kime-nage, sumi-otoshi, jyuji-nage, hiki-otoshi, sukui-nage,* and so on. Some schools incorporate more armlocks, some have more hip and shoulder throws, a few even include trips, sweeps (of foot) and reaps (of thigh), and others include punches and kicks. Obviously, the greater the number of techniques that are included, the more the art begins to resemble Jujutsu. But exactly what is it that defines Aikido? Most Aikido schools restrict themselves to a fairly limited number of techniques. Some speak of techniques that do not match their philosophy, others believe that their own school's syllabus represents the totality of Aikido, claiming it to be a complete system, and so on and so forth. What defines a particular brand of Aikido lies in the principles used. Each teacher absorbs a slightly different set of principles based on his own learning experience and ultimately these principles become reflected in his style or individual teaching method.

Udekime-nage.

Sumi-otoshi.

Jyuji-nage.

Hiki-otoshi.

Wrist hold.

Technical Progress Chart

In many schools of Aikido, beginners are often bamboozled by the seemingly random multitude of techniques. In the early days of Aikido in Europe, a system was adopted along the lines of *first form = ai-hanmi katate-dori, second form = gyaku-hanmi katate-dori,* and so on. For the first grading, students would typically have to demonstrate all the basic techniques,

about ten of them, from a first form attack. For the second grading they had to do both *first* and *second forms,* and so on. Some schools still use this system and by the time students reach *Shodan,* the knowledge attained is more or less equivalent to that of the complicated-looking Aikikai or Yoshinkan syllabuses.

If this seems to be a bit of a mess, one way of making sense of it is for students to make a kind of Aikido multiplication table. Write the basic techniques at the top of the columns, and the attacks along the rows. If you want, you could divide each box into two or three to account for *tachi-waza, hanmi-handachi-waza* and *suwari-waza*. As your learning progresses, the chart is filled in and you can always see immediately where the gaps are. The curious student could try to work out unknowns using *aiki* principles with a co-operative *uke*.

Aikido Progress Chart

Basic Attacks Techniques	Ai-hanmi katate-dori	Gyaku-hanmi katate-dori	Sode-dori	Mune-dori	Shomen-uchi	Yokomen-uchi	Tsuki	Ushiro ryote-dori
Kokyu-irimi								
Kokyu-tenkan								
Ikkyo								
Nikyo								
Sankyo								
Yonkyo								
Gokyo								
Irimi-nage								
Shiho-nage								
Kote-gaeshi								
Kaiten-nage								
Tenchi-nage								

An improved method of memory retention is to base one's techniques on principles found in specific *kokyu-nage* for each attack. For example, choose one method of *kokyu-nage* to represent an *irimi* movement and then try to base the *irimi* versions of the following techniques upon that movement. Do likewise for *tenkan*.

15 Advanced Techniques

If I have seen farther than others, it is because I was standing on the shoulders of giants. *Isaac Newton*

It could be argued that a straight punch is an advanced technique in Judo, *ikkyo* is an advanced technique in Karate, and a front kick is an advanced technique in Aikido. A technique that is commonly considered to be advanced in one art may be basic in another. Rather than any technique being advanced, it is usually the case that less emphasis is placed on it. Simply, if a student practises it frequently, it will be easy. Accordingly, there are no 'advanced' techniques, only the student's own narrow experience.

Secret Techniques

No matter how much the teacher tries to reveal, if the student is not ready to receive, the 'secret' remains invisible. An open but often unmentioned secret is the addition of *atemi* to Aikido techniques. For example, in the midst of *shomen-uchi* and *yokomen-uchi ikkyo*, it is possible to add two powerful *atemi* without interfering with the flow of movement. A low kick or trip could also be incorporated.

The Twenty-Year Technique

Some jokingly refer to *ikkyo* as the 'twenty-year technique'. In some senses this is true since, over time, there is a change in the way the student approaches it; it becomes more personalized with experience yet never solidifies in form. Rather, the secret of *ikkyo* is in escaping the form; those who

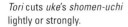

Shomen-uchi ikkyo.

Tori cuts *uke*'s *shomen-uchi* lightly or strongly.

Shomen-uchi ikkyo
(continued).

Tori strikes the floating ribs.

Tori strikes the face.

Tori moves into standard
ikkyo.

Yokomen-uchi ikkyo.

Tori hits *uke*'s *yokomen-uchi* lightly or strongly.

Tori parries with a hitting feeling.

Tori strikes the floating ribs.

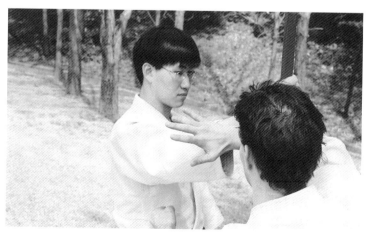

Yokomen-uchi ikkyo (continued).

Tori strikes the face.

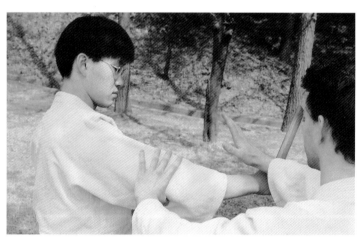

Tori moves into standard *ikkyo*.

stick to the absolute form will never learn it, even after fifty years. The perfection of the form blinds them. This is not only true of *ikkyo*, but of Aikido in general. If the student fails to graduate from the *shu* of *shu-ha-ri*, he will never escape the basic form. This contrasts starkly with O Sensei, since his post-war Aikido life was spent enjoying the *ri* of *shu-ha-ri*.

In order to escape, you need to think for yourself. Of course, the main reason it takes so long is because there is no one there to guide. O Sensei's path was personal and is impossible to follow. The modern *kata*-based syllabuses of various schools appear to lack logical progression to freedom, so it is left for the self to discover. Some do, many do not, but there is no need to wait for twenty years to try.

Henka-Waza
Depending on the school, the idea of modifying technique ranges from being totally unacceptable to being absolutely essential. Some schools keep their students to a strict syllabus, others teach what they label as *henka-waza* in addition to standard techniques. Few schools encourage their

Ikkyo, elbow hand palm-up.

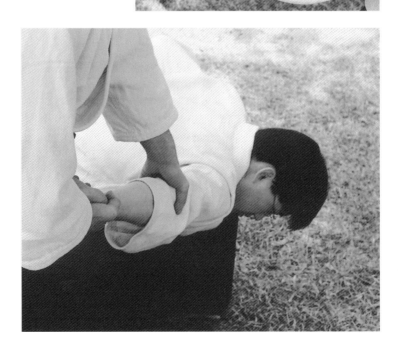

RIGHT: *Ikkyo*, elbow hand with reverse grip from behind.

Ikkyo, elbow hand with reverse grip from side.

Irimi-nage variation.

Nikyo variation.

Koshi-nage variation.

students to experiment by themselves, which almost sums up the totality of more practical arts such as Judo. Following principles found within the various techniques, it is not too difficult for the average student to come up with new blends on more traditional shapes.

Renraku-Waza

The basic techniques that were left by O Sensei are quite interesting. Aikido does not have nearly so many techniques as other arts, but there do seem to be enough to twist an arm or throw a body in a multitude of ways. Generally, in Aikido, a great deal of emphasis is placed on getting the technique right. Not much thought is given to combinations, or to mixing different techniques together – at least, that is, according to the syllabus. What happens is that, once you have enough experience, it starts to happen naturally. For example, if you throw *uke* down with *kote-gaeshi*, without turning him over, you can let him get up a little, move around to his rear, and begin *irimi-nage*. It just fits perfectly. Once the basics are mastered, combinations pour out, yet they are rarely taught. Clearly, O Sensei's choice of basic techniques is remarkable in the sense that, with a little thought, they all link together naturally.

Kaeshi-Waza

What is interesting is that the same principles used to make technique can also be used to counter, to make *kaeshi-waza*, reversing the technique upon *uke*. Not quite as easy as combinations, and rarely practised, they first appear as new techniques to be learned. However, since they work according to the same *aiki* principles, it does not take long for the initiated to realize that a little 'unbendable arm' when receiving technique goes a long way towards making an effective counter. You should not overly resist or struggle when performing counters. *Uke* should give *tori* something to work with, and *tori* should find a way to use it without resorting to strained effort.

One useful example is to let *uke* do *nikyo*. *Tori* should be after *uke*'s downward motion at the point of application, just at the point of pain. He gives his (right) wrist almost completely to *uke*. As *uke* applies the pain, *tori* lowers his body and arm together matching *uke*'s movement exactly, but leading *uke*'s energy with his wrist he overtakes *uke*'s movement. Then, as he stands back up, he instantly has a *kote-gaeshi* grip on *uke* using his left hand, working through *uke*'s thumb using his right forearm. The trick is not to resist at all, but to blend with, add to, and overtake *uke*'s movement. Of course, if *uke* knows what *tori* is going to do in advance, the *nikyo* might be applied much more sharply. In that case, *tori* may not give his wrist quite so completely.

Once an interest in *kaeshi-waza* is aroused, the student should begin to collect enough to deal with the various Aikido techniques.

Pressure Points

Every beginner expects that at some point they are going to learn the secret pressure points of Aikido. There is a problem here in that they remain secret because no one knows them. They do not exist in any regular Aikido syllabus, but they do indeed exist. If you are shown one, make sure you remember it, and begin your collection. The easiest way to learn pressure points is to train at a school that teaches an art that uses them regularly, such as Jujutsu. With a little ingenuity, *aikidoka* will be able to apply them in their Aikido techniques; the key is to try to make them fit into the

Thumb in eye.

Fingers around trachea.

Punch to solar plexus.

technique, not to make the technique fit the pressure point. As an added benefit, you will know where your own weak points are and thus be on better guard.

Strangles and Chokes

Strangling stops the flow of blood to the brain, while choking refers to closing the windpipe, preventing breathing. Both can be done with the bare hands or arms, or by grabbing the collar(s) of the *keikogi*. Variations can be done from the front, the side or the rear. Although they are not normally done in Aikido, some teachers do show them from time to time. The student ought to keep a note and record the various methods; there is no point in being a passive learner for material that is not on the syllabus. Otherwise, the only option is to go to Judo or Jujutsu classes to learn their *shime-waza*. Practising Aikido techniques against simple strangles and chokes offers a more sensible self-defence perspective.

Non-Aikido Techniques

Many of the techniques in other arts can be done according to *aiki* principles, so there are few techniques that are specifically 'non-Aikido'. Such techniques might appear advanced to the uninitiated, but they are often quickly picked up by the co-ordinated *aikidoka*. Indeed, if *aiki* can be added to a technique, then it can be called Aikido. A trip or sweep practised with solid *aiki* contact and harmony can be called good *aiki*, even though the form might look like Judo.

Aiki is sometimes apparent in other arts even though it is not taught as a principle.

Front collar strangle.

Osoto-gari.

Kosoto-gari.

Ouchi-gari.

Kouchi-gari.

Kata-seoi-otoshi.

Ude-gatame.

Some Karate and Judo teachers have great *aiki* within. Their *aiki* has developed naturally through hard training, but they cannot pass it on to their students since they do not know they have it, and they cannot even give it a name. Anyway, the crux is that any technique can be an *aiki* technique if it follows *aiki* principles; it is not limited to Aikido form.

Randori

In Shodokan Aikido there is competition that by necessity has rules – for example, one of the rules stipulates no tripping – but it makes sense to be interested in what you are not allowed to do. There are many occasions when a trip is an excellent choice of technique. Such 'shapes' appear constantly in the bustle of *randori*, so it is advisable to reserve the rules for competition, not for training. Whatever the style of Aikido, if it claims to be a martial art then there is no way it can justify not being able to use the occasional Judo throw or Karate strike, especially if they are applied using *aiki* principles.

16 *Ukemi*

If you don't stand for something you will fall for anything.
Malcolm X

In Aikido, *uke* is regarded as a partner and is someone you train with, not someone you train on. It is an enigmatic theory perhaps, but the better you carry out the role of *uke* the better your own Aikido will become. If you are just waiting for your turn to do the technique, then it will be very difficult for you to learn Aikido.

Movement

Jumping through the air and falling is not what is meant by *ukemi* in Aikido. It is certainly good training, and students should practise falling and getting up in a solid forward, central, or rear posture facing forwards in the direction of travel or from the direction from whence they came. Many variations on this can be made, but it is still not what is sought. *Ukemi* is the receipt of technique – you must be immobilized or thrown to truly receive.

When receiving technique, the movement should emanate from the body's centre. Do not collapse or fall over without good reason, nor jump before being thrown. In the beginning, learn to go wherever *tori* leads, lightly but firmly, and without any apprehension. Next, get past the stage of knowing where you are going to fall – learn to trust *tori*. Skill at being *uke* is the single most important factor in determining your *aiki* potential.

Flying *uke*s are fun to train with but one must never fall into the trap of believing it

is your own skill that makes them fly – it is theirs, and if you want that skill, you must fly too. Most of the criticism directed towards Aikido concerns practice where *uke*s appear to fly too easily. The smart *aikidoka* knows that it is but one method of practice where *uke* might be flying in anticipation of avoiding an incoming strike. Doing it is exhilarating but students must not stray too far from the basics. You need to add energy actively to the attack and throw *uke* most of the time. Those *uke*s who clamp on to *tori*'s wrist hard and resist all movement are usually doing what some jokingly call 'aiki Judo'. Judo is an active art, in which technique is made on *uke*, and *kuzushi* and *tsukuri*, or actively breaking balance and making technique, are involved. Of course, it is possible to practise Aikido that way too but it is not ideal. If *uke* decides to clamp on hard it is imperative for him to press in and contact *tori*'s centre, thereby creating a real attack. *Uke* is not dead meat; *uke* should not just hang on to *tori*; *uke* is alive.

It is important to train realistically so that, when you are attacked by the stereotypical knife-wielding madman, harmony will emerge from the chaos. Of course, if technique is lacking and the madman runs out of steam before his attack has a chance to work, there is nothing wrong in using all available strength to take full advantage of the lull in his attack – just recognize that this is not the perfection that is sought.

Receiving Learning

Taking *Ukemi* means to receive technique but in Aikido the role of *uke* is far more important than just that. *Uke* has to attack *tori* so completely that *uke* is in fact giving himself to *tori* to play with. *Tori* learns to deal with this attacking energy, redirecting it this way or that. Put simply, if there is no attack, there can be no technique in Aikido. *Tori* is not doing the technique on *uke*, rather, *uke* is doing it to himself. This is the ideal, but in a more realistic scenario, *tori* and *uke* produce about 50 per cent of the technique between them. What commonly happens is that *uke*'s energy runs out mid-technique, *tori* swings him around, and then splats him into the *tatami* – not quite perfect. Instead, *uke*'s energy should be active for the whole time for good *aiki* to develop. In this case, *tori* has overtaken *uke* and taken the lead, and it could be argued that the roles have changed; *uke* should therefore have defended against *tori*'s uninvited input of energy. Yet this is the way students usually practise.

Worse still, if there is no real attack, then *tori* has to do all of the technique on *uke*. The problem is with the attack, or, in other words, with *uke*. After the initial attack is over, *uke* should continue to press into *tori*, thereby maintaining contact. It is correct for *tori* to add energy to *uke*'s attack but the emphasis here is on adding to something that is already extant. If there is no attack, or the attack peters out, there is nothing to add to. It is over.

The secret to developing your *aiki* as *tori* is to become a good responsive *uke* since it is in this role that you will realize how your energy is being manipulated. Accordingly, an alive, responsive *uke* will improve as *tori*. For example, when receiving technique from a senior, *uke* has direct input, remembers what happens, and tries to replicate it when becoming *tori*. A student gains far more insight in receiving technique as *uke* than by performing it as *tori*.

Submission

When receiving pain it is important for *uke* not to grimace or shout uncontrollably. The expression should be normal and controlled, and the tap signals the pain. *Uke* uses two quick taps to signal to *tori* that he either cannot move, or that his pain limit has been reached. With a simple immobilization such as *ikkyo* there is often no pain. In this case, *uke* tries to get up, fails, and signals this to *tori* by tapping; *tori* then releases. If there is pain, *uke* signals with two quick taps and *tori* releases.

Two taps are given because that signifies deliberate decision. A simple tap could be mistaken for general noise within the midst of technique, such as when *uke* hits the floor with his hand or body when break-falling. If possible, *uke* taps against *tori*'s arm, leg or body as this transmits the message best. Failing that, *uke* taps against his own leg or body or, if lying prone, he taps the floor.

Uke Behaviour

When taking *ukemi* it is important to breathe. Holding the breath promotes stiffness and this is easily detected by *tori*. There are many things to remember when training yet some students actually stop breathing when practising. Instead of breathing naturally their breath becomes something akin to a grunt. To get over this problem, it is important always to emphasize breathing out when practising breakfalls. Next, from, say, *koshi-nage*, practise breathing out sharply when hitting the floor. *Tori* can even jump down on *uke*'s chest, body-to-body, Judo style, just after *uke* lands, necessitating another sharp outward breath by *uke* for his own self-protection. *Tori* also breathes out to make the hit.

Uke should continually try to get up, albeit gently. If *tori* leaves a *suki* then *uke* should respond accordingly. *Uke* could simply escape, deliver *atemi*, counter, or just get up. For example, the pain of a wristlock such as *nikyo* drives *uke* down, but if released *uke* should be up immediately. After being fully immobilized on the ground, on release *uke* should get up quickly; in fact, *uke* should aim to get up before *tori*, and *tori* should aim to prevent this by getting up first.

When repeatedly getting up off of the floor, *uke* should maintain composure and alertness, and not look exhausted. When tired, he should just stop. He should strive not to look tired, and should keep the breathing in rhythm. A good teacher ought to spot when a student is tired and act accordingly. Training in this way will enable the student to become immune to the shock of sudden pain; giving the impression of being able to bear it more will instil in an opponent an amount of uncertainty or self-doubt.

The responsive *aiki* feeling between *tori* and *uke* also allows a psychological understanding to develop. You will instinctively know if your partner is happy, apprehensive, nervous, or none of these. Aikido develops this and, after time, practitioners will be better able to gauge the feelings of others outside of the *dojo*. Finally, a good *uke* is someone who would use his common sense for the simple avoidance of a life-threatening situation.

17 Weapons

I don't know with what weapons World War III will be fought, but World War IV will be fought with sticks and stones.
Albert Einstein

To learn to use weapons, the student needs to see many teachers, if only because many of them have little skill. Daggers, swords and staves are no longer part of modern culture, and as a result it is rare to find people who truly know about them; modern *Karateka* busily practising their *kama* (sickle) *kata* would probably tire of cutting grass after ten minutes.

It is commonly believed that the point of weapons training in Aikido is to improve the empty-hand techniques. With this in mind, since many of Aikido's basic movements are based upon sword-related principles, it certainly makes sense to practise using a sword; the enigma remains, of course, since a student could devote a lifetime of study to this weapon itself.

Bokken

The usual method of holding a *bokken* is hands spread one fist-width apart to gain a measure of leverage when cutting. Another way that exists in Japanese arts is to hold the *bokken* as if holding a baseball bat, with the hands close together. While swinging the *bokken* and cutting, the hands-spread method dictates that the swordsman punches slightly with the upper hand and pulls with the lower at the point of striking. The feeling of cutting is also akin to the back-pull of a saw. (Interestingly, the Japanese saw cuts with the back-pull, unlike the Western saw, which cuts with

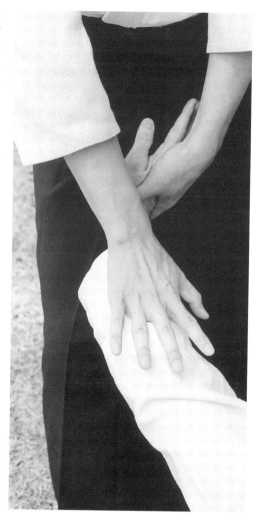

Cutting up and down with *uke*'s arm creates Aikido techniques.

Both *tori* and *uke* keep centre.

the push.) So, the sword enters the opponent's body at the shoulder, cuts down, and then comes out, as if taking a large slice; it is not a slash, but a definite cut. With a fast cut, hitting with the end 2–3in (5–7cm) of the blade the sword may snick in and out in a moment; in a heavy, slower, deeper cut, the body weight is added to the upper hand, to increase the power or depth of the cut or, rather, slice.

When cutting with the sword in Aikido it is important to match the cut to your body movement. For *shomen-uchi* the body moves forwards or back when cutting. With *yokomen-uchi* it may seem that the body moves sideways as you cut. This should not happen. In fact, you turn and, when cutting, although the cut is diagonal to the temple or neck area, the body moves forwards or back, straight, just as in *shomen-uchi*. Some schools cut *kesa*, a large diagonal cut down the line of the *keikogi*, with the blade finishing near the *tatami*. Even in this case, if you are carried around by the momentum of the strike, it is not correct. When cutting, think of *torifune*. Cut forwards.

When practising with a weapon it is necessary to have a vivid imagination, a sense of what is really supposed to be happening.

While it appears to be the norm to run through various *kata* or sequences of techniques, the real nitty-gritty of training is basic – holding centre, evasion, cutting, and thrusting. After each movement the tip of the weapon must return instantly to point towards uke, otherwise the centre will be lost.

It is vital to practise against single cuts coming from a single direction and to train in various responses:

• avoiding left or right, moving close enough to hit at the right time with an appropriate stroke;
• moving just out of range, but not so far that a counter is impossible;
• after barely avoiding, there may be a need to parry;
• after avoiding well, there is no need to parry at all, just strike.

If there is no avoidance, you must block, but being defensive, *uke* may gain the control of rhythm. Instead of the block it is possible to use the counter-strike, or forceful parry. This can be done with or without avoiding, and has the effect of dashing *uke*'s sword back, as in *irimi*, or out, as in *tenkan*. Sometimes, a forceful parry can also turn into a counter-strike in the same stroke, especially if the avoiding body movement has a forward component.

Attacks are parried using the flat, or the back ridge. The blade edge could be used directly against a wooden weapon with the intention of cutting it, but not against a sword. When using the flat you have to push, not hit, otherwise your own sword could be broken. It is better to use the back ridge by forcefully twisting your sword against *uke*'s. Done sharply, this has

Focus on *uke*.

Being focused upon.

Standard downblow.

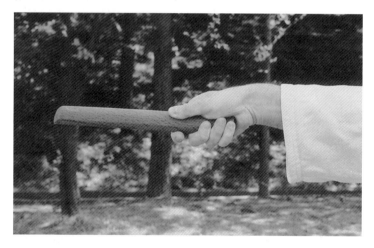

Standard thrust.

the effect of dashing *uke*'s sword away while protecting the edge.

The student should also experiment with transferring these movements to the *jo* and, of course, to the empty-hand techniques.

Jo

To maximize the thrust distance the *jo* is held with the little finger feeling the end, with the other hand about one-third of the way along. When performing Aikido-type techniques on *uke* it is sometimes held with a few inches protruding from the

lower hand – this is useful for hooking an arm or wrist, or the neck. At other times it is held and used like a *bokken*, striking the opponent with the tip.

As with the *bokken*, it makes sense to practise avoiding, moving and responding in all possible directions. Obviously different from the *bokken*, the *jo* has two ends and is not sharp, but all of the same principles apply. It goes without saying that when training you should always try to hit and receive ever faster and harder. The imperative necessity to avoid adds a measure of reality to maintaining both mental composure and good technique under violent duress. For training in a sharp counter-strike, especially one with minimal or no avoidance, it is better to start with the *jo* than with the *bokken*. Using the *jo*, the hands are typically held further apart than with the *bokken*; this adds a measure of control that helps the student to learn the principle while at the same time maintaining a degree of safety.

Practice should be carried out on both left and right sides for dexterity, and this is more likely to be done with the *jo* than the *bokken* in most *dojo*s.

Tanto

There are four ways to hold the single-bladed *tanto*. In a straight, forward thrust, the blade can point upwards or downwards. For the downward stab, the blade likewise has two positions. For standard thrusting in Aikido, the blade should be pointed upwards. While the *tanto* is made of wood only, you should imagine that the thrust has a degree of upward motion that cuts upwards through the fleshy parts just below the ribs and up towards the heart. It is not so much a stab as an upward, singular, saw-like cut. In the downward blow the blade should be facing you and you should have your thumb over the end to prevent slippage – Japanese *tanto*s usually have no *tsuba* (blade guard). When striking, it not only stabs but also cuts as it enters, and, once it has entered deeply, rather than withdraw it the way it went in, you could draw it back towards yourself while cutting upwards slightly, thereby causing more damage. It may not be nice, but that is the way it is practised in Aikido. The *tanto* blade could be reversed but then your thrusting technique would have to be modified accordingly. For example, in the forward thrust, you would have to cut downwards slightly, not up.

Since the *tanto* is the weapon that is most relevant to modern times, *aikidoka* naturally need to practise all Aikido techniques against *tanto* attacks from all possible directions. The direction of the strike often determines the pattern of avoidance and the nature of the technique, so is easy for a smart *tori* to predict. The problem is that the *tanto* is a weapon based on hand movement, not on body movement. Typically, an *aikidoka* attacks in the standard way, putting his body weight behind the movement, so there is no problem – except that it is less realistic. To broaden his scope, *tori* needs to practise moving in at least a couple of different directions for each type of strike. However, this will obviously not work against a weapon based on hand movement, since the hand moves much faster than the body. Since Aikido technique depends on body movement, to deal with a fast *tanto*, an *aikidoka* has to learn to use the hands to deflect and/or take an arm before a solid Aikido technique can be applied. Here, an understanding of timing and the willingness to take a cut are crucial to success.

Many Aikido techniques are performed against *tanto* attack. In each case, the distance and technique vary slightly. Some techniques on the syllabus are not sensible, and the keen student needs to maintain a discerning eye. For practical self-defence it makes good sense to develop a private collection of effective techniques based on simplicity and effectiveness. *Tori* can also take the *tanto* and apply *aiki* techniques with it in either hand.

When training with *uke*, the practitioner typically takes the weapon and leaves it on the floor at a distance so that *uke* has to get up and take at least a step to retrieve it. Alternatively, it is taken away and handed back. The polite way to hand over a *tanto* (or *bokken*) is with the blade

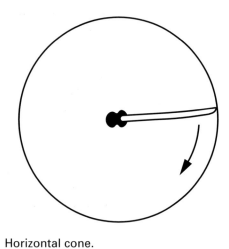

Horizontal cone.

LEFT: Vertical cone.

towards yourself and the handle away from your own strong hand, showing trust.

Vertical or Horizontal Spirals

Holding a *bokken* or *jo* vertically and drawing a circle above the head with the point creates a cone shape. The same can be done holding the sword out horizontally. Combining this movement with forward, or sometimes rear or sideways, body movement creates a spiral. Spiral movements are very powerful and can be used for defence or attack with *bokken* and *jo* alike. When doing this, your centre should always move in unison with the bottom (handle) of the weapon.

Mixing It Up

Empty hand against sword is fun but unrealistic: first, it is probably never going to

happen in modern society; second, the unarmed person would almost certainly be cut down instantly against a real swordsman. Empty hand against a staff is more plausible. Empty hand against a knife could be the reality waiting around the next corner.

Bokken against *jo* is also fun. While it is almost never going to happen outside the *dojo*, it is useful to practise with weapons of differing lengths. The first key to overcoming any weapon is to know its strengths and weaknesses by using it. Therefore the key to any form of mixed practice is always in the basics; if your basics are good, you may just have a chance when that sword-wielding lunatic jumps out in front of you.

Finally, it is obvious that the more strongly you strike and receive in *bokken* or *jo* training, the better the practice. You can negotiate the terms with *uke* and really batter each other quite hard with safety. Accordingly, the occasional broken weapon in training can be considered as good practice. However, when training empty hand against *jo*, or performing *kokyu-nage* using the *jo*, a breakage is indicative of bad technique.

Footwork

One of the main advantages of cutting and thrusting with the *bokken* and *jo* in Aikido is that the footwork contained in the various patterns almost immediately transfers over to your empty-hand techniques. To improve your avoidance, cutting, and idea of space all at the same time, it is imperative to move more. For example, rather than the standard one-step, one-cut routines seen in many *dojos*, try walking forwards and cutting once every right step. This is cutting every second step. Of course, it makes sense to do likewise on the left step. Next, walk forwards and cut every third step. This time, the cut will occur on alternating feet. These routines can be done at a slow, brisk or fast pace. Side, back and rear avoiding movements can also be incorporated. Cutting in various degrees of *taisabaki* also helps. This can be done with *shomen-uchi*, *yokomen-uchi*, *do* and *tsuki*. In addition, practising blocks and parries will give *tori* a greater feeling of control over a wider area.

Building a Framework

Many schools practise *bokken* and *jo kata*, yet fail to make any connections between the individual techniques found within, which could otherwise lead a keen student to a more complete understanding of the weapon at hand.

When facing *uke*, you can theoretically cut in any number of directions around a clock face and thrust *jodan*, *chudan* or *gedan* along a left, right or central plane. In reality, after avoiding a certain strike in a certain direction at a certain time, only one defensive option and counter-strike will commonly be available; at most, there may be two. Less choice means less hesitation but it also makes it easier for a wise opponent to know what is coming. The most important point in learning is to build a framework of patterns of movement that are easy to visualize for the self and easy to recognize in an opponent.

The easiest way to remember all the different attacking strokes is to cut around an imaginary clock. Twelve o'clock represents *shomen-uchi*. Eleven and one o'clock represent *yokomen-uchi* or *kesa*. Nine and three o'clock represent *do*, the midsection. Seven and five o'clock represent upward rising cuts. Six o'clock is a vertical upward cut. These same attacking movements and directions can also be turned to the defensive. Putting body weight behind the blow and transferring the energy into the opponent's weapon can have a blocking, parrying or intercepting counter-strike effect. Naturally, it makes sense to imagine being attacked from those same directions when practising defensive moves. What matters is that the mind thinks for itself and creates sense out of the spurious myriad of *kata* techniques. Do not wait to be taught – it might never happen.

Holding the sword vertically, somewhat similar to *hasso*, you can rotate it around in a horizontal axis either clockwise, or anticlockwise. Using this, you can deflect incoming *yokomen-uchi* by adding firm energy to the movement at the moment of contact. The closer to the hilt the blow is received, the more leverage you have and the easier it is to deflect. However, the whole point of having a long weapon is to take advantage of the operational distance it provides. Therefore, you need to develop the ability to deflect strong blows using a point closer to the tip, typically working your way up to a point about one-third of the way down from the point, or two-thirds up from the hilt. In this case, lacking leverage to develop power, you need to use speed, timing and courage. The opponent's sword must be met mid-swing at full speed, and at that point of meeting, additional heavier energy must be momentarily added to strike or dash away the incoming blow. Striking it contains a greater speed element; dashing has a slightly slower speed component, but is heavier. Furthermore, depending upon whether it was a clockwise or anti-clockwise rotation, the result might be either a forceful parry or an intercepting counter-strike. Similar patterns can be developed for other attacks around the 'clock'.

Once you have a collection of distinct strikes and defences, after practising footwork and body movement in eight directions, natural avoidance and attack patterns reveal themselves. For example, moving to the rear left corner you are obviously defending your right side. If your own sword tip is down, it invites attack from above; if your tip is up, it invites attack from below. Here, you can respond by either raising or lowering the sword, respectively, and making an appropriate defence and/or counter-strike. Accordingly, using the principles acquired in *kata* and using them while moving in each of the eight directions, you will begin to see how they all fit together.

Another method to build a framework is to connect blocks and strikes together in pairs. The simplest exercise for this is to parry *shomen-uchi* with *kaeshi-men* while avoiding to the side. Next, attack *shomen-uchi* while your partner parries in the same way. If the parries are always done on the same side, you will traverse in a circle. If both alternate left and right each time, you will return to the same spot every two techniques. This kind of exercise can be repeated over and over, with speed and power being slowly added. With a little imagination, many more of the basic techniques can be practised in pairs in this way. What is more, their simplicity allows increased vigour, which leads to more reality. These same exercises can be done with the *jo*. The diversity of the *jo*, however, leads to even more interesting routines just waiting to be re-discovered.

18 *Aiki*

The reasonable man adapts himself to the world; the unreasonable one persists in trying to adapt the world to himself. *George Bernard Shaw*

O Sensei's Aikido moved away from the traditional static *kata*-based approach towards a style that was more a living entity – a responsive art that has as its basis a feeling of unison between *tori* and *uke*. While *uke* makes attack, *tori* harmonizes to the extent that any movement of *tori*'s centre corresponds to movement in *uke*'s centre. A few have this from their very first day of training even though they might not realize it; most take much longer and some never achieve it.

Realm of the Possible
The ultimate in *aiki* power is that lone finger, quite incomprehensible, that steers *uke* up and away or down to the floor with delicate precision. A contrasting method is to send *uke* away or down with such a force, again with seemingly little effort, that he is momentarily shocked and experiences sudden fear. It is impossible for most practitioners to do and even for the students of those who can. It will be necessary to travel far and wide to seek and experience it – if only to know the realm of the possible and to keep it in mind as a distant aim. In the meantime, every student needs to develop a more practical and achievable definition of what *aiki* is.

Defining Practice
The *yin/yang* duality of Chinese thought can be applied to the *aiki* learning approach. The smaller the eyes of the *yin/yang* circles, the greater the difference between the hard and soft, either between styles, or within a style – but, even though the eyes are small, hardness remains as an intrinsic part of softness and vice versa. The larger the eyes, the more the two merge into each other, meeting at some happy median. Even within a style there are always those of a slightly harder or softer disposition than others. At one extreme are those who use only solid technique from a strong centre to twirl *uke* around and down; at the other extreme are those who insist that *uke*'s determined attack must be the sole energy input leading to his demise. In reality, a student's favourite training partners will be those who are most like him. When dealing with extremes of any kind, it makes sense to bring the majority towards the centre by developing *aikidoka* with 'large eyes'. However, this does not mean that the 'little eyes' are wrong – working at the extremes is absolutely necessary, and it is a mistake to work at only one.

Progressive Method
There are two common poles from which to start the *aiki* journey. The first route recommends 'light-fast' training. This develops rapid understanding of movement, timing and co-ordination. The

Big eyes.

Little eyes.

second path is a 'slow-heavy' approach, through which the student learns to perform basic movements against increasing resistance practising with many different people. Both routes have validity and head towards the same destination, yet many practitioners – perhaps most – never arrive. In the meantime, adding a component of slow heaviness later to the 'light-fast' route is not easy, as that student has always trained to be light, and this will seem to run against the perceived *aiki* grain. In contrast, adding speed to the 'slow-heavy' approach instils the idea of logical advancement in skill.

While in the short term progress seems to be slow, in the long run it leads to a better understanding of the basics; training against measured resistance means that, by necessity, *tori* has to contact with *uke*'s centre from the very beginning of his *aiki* journey. By adding speed later, *tori* can create and maintain the *aiki* feeling that has already been learned within more rapid movement. Natural progression is surely the logical means: adding speed to heaviness later on in your development is

far more beneficial than trying to add heaviness to speed.

The most important fact is that someone who does not have *aiki* can be taught to recognize it and to develop it and the most efficient means of doing this is through solid *kokyu-ho* and *kokyu-nage* exercises. Students first learn to move *uke* from a position of mechanical strength and over time the aim is to advance by reducing the amount of effort needed, replacing force with technical skill amidst the harmony of fluid movement. To achieve this, it is necessary to develop a composite understanding of co-ordination, space, time, speed, power and technical skill – all realistic aims in the quest for understanding. True *aiki* appears when *tori* demonstrates superb sensitivity in movement, merging with *uke*'s strike or grip and general body movement to the extent that *uke* actually feels comfortable while being immobilized or thrown. However, it is also necessary to learn how to disrupt and cause disharmony and imbalance in *uke*, sometimes to the extent that he feels very uncomfortable.

With any logical approach, even if *aiki* were never fully understood, the keen student should still have a good understanding of martial movement resulting in real skill in self-defence. The point here is that achievable aims need to be set, worked on and overcome. If the only aim is one-finger magical Aikido there will be no practical means to achieve it. At each level of development, your understanding of *aiki* will necessarily change; there is no singular answer as to what it is in the midst of process, only that you should seek it, all the while keeping an eye on that elusive goal, while never straying too far from reality.

Other *Aiki*

Definitions of *aiki* can be broadened to include any means whereby *uke* is controlled or toppled with minimal effort. For example, any efficient means of taking *uke*'s balance to effect an immobilization or projection can be regarded as being in tune with *uke* and as such, it will not be limited only to Aikido. Tripping someone up requires perfect timing and co-ordination, and the result is an unbalanced *uke* who is momentarily wide open for a technique. A boxer who can avoid all attacks with ease and hit his opponent at will is demonstrating a kind of *aiki*. The magician who misleads his subjects, directing their attention almost at will, performs an excellent composite of mental and physical skills in the moment. The husband/wife, worker/boss and man/dog who accurately gauge the mind or feelings of the other with careful observation are somehow in tune with each other; this kind of skill can be an example of *aiki*. Extending the argument further, any craftsman who is master of his trade and can do some complicated-looking task with nonchalant effort is also demonstrating a form of *aiki* between himself and the object on which he is working.

Encompass All

Aiki cannot be found by practising external technique alone. In the broad sense, you have to collect together and develop all the principles of Aikido. *Aiki*, in essence, is the flow of energy, thus *tori* has to learn to flow with, and to take control of, *uke*'s energy. The purpose of doing this is to defeat *uke* in a martial sense – it is not a dance, nor is it peaceful. Aikido uses the *tegatana* and, as such, various hand positions become very important. However, while the *tegatana* is a useful tool for learning to understand *aiki*, it is not the be-all and end-all of technique. Those who understand *aiki* do not need a strong *tegatana* to demonstrate it. The most common method of learning *aiki* is in terms of physical hand-to-hand contact, but this is only one of several means available to redirect *uke*'s energy; patience brings solution, calmness dissipates anger, confidence instils doubt, *kiai* shocks, *atemi*, real or feint, causes reaction – all need consideration.

Regardless of the Way you are following, the key to arriving at the destination is planning your own journey. You need to know where you are at, where you are going, what you need to continue, and how to get it. It is not good enough to rely on others. It is important to realize that there are no shortcuts, no magic grips or hand positions, and no secret escapes; the only real way is through consistent hard training while consciously incorporating and unifying all the aspects of Aikido over an extended period of time.

19 Methods of Practice

A wise man will make more opportunities than he finds.
Sir Francis Bacon

Rather than have hundreds of techniques, the aim of Aikido is to develop the few to a high standard. In doing this, it is fortunate that there are many different methods of practice. For example, in theory, all the techniques on the syllabus can be done from *suwari-waza*, *hanmi-handachi-waza* or *tachi-waza*. Also, many of the basic movements can be duplicated in weapon work. There are also several other useful methods of practice.

Kata

O Sensei eventually abandoned the *kata* approach to learning that he had known in Daito-ryu. In contrast, some of his pre-war students, such as Tomiki Kenji (Shodokan) and Shioda Gozo (Yoshinkan), maintained a more *kata*-based approach for their Aikido schools.

Kata sets are often performed on one side only. In traditional Ryu, the practitioner was usually right-handed and carried a sword at his left side, so all techniques were performed with that in mind. This is a sensible approach for self-defence since too many choices might serve to confuse. In Shodokan Aikido the *kata* are collections of general techniques or principles. The purpose of performing the *kata* is for the students to show their teachers that they understand the principles. Beyond that, the *kata* techniques form a resource library; it is up to the students to visit that library, to borrow, think about and practise all the techniques on both sides where necessary. The most important point to discern from *kata* is not the technique itself but the principle it represents. It is a mistake to seek *aiki* in the *kata* performed as a set.

Kata are usually regarded as unchanging sets of techniques. Typically, in any one *kata* set every technique is different. Often, the order is organized for the benefit of convenience; in the *randori-no-kata* of Shodokan, every technique is performed in right posture from a rising *shomen-uchi*. Some will be content to leave it at that, but the more curious will try it on the left side, or from different attacks. Contrasting this, Shodokan's *koryu-no-kata* mix left- and right-sided techniques together – if *tori* finishes in left posture, then the next technique often begins from that position, and so on. Judo's most basic *kata* set, *nage-no-kata*, is performed on both sides, but other Judo *kata*s are generally practised in the traditional way, on one side only, sometimes the right, sometimes the left.

In Yoshinkan, the meticulous training regimen means that every technique could be regarded as an unchanging individual *kata* that is practised on both sides. Iwama Ryu (Saito Morihiro) is not quite as rigid as Yoshinkan but its regimen still requires strong conformity. In Aikikai, there is more variety of method between schools and more variation in style is accepted but, in essence, each technique is still performed more or less as an individual *kata*.

The *kata* sets of the various martial arts are often used to train a certain technical grouping or to inoculate a certain mental spirit. Some are to be done fast and furious, some demonstrate certain principles, some work on concentration, others demonstrate flow, others demonstrate self-defence applications, and so on. Practising *kata* sets in series to perfection seems to be the intended purpose for many, but the fact is that you have to practise the techniques out of the *kata* set to learn them properly. Shodokan students often practise whole sets. Yoshinkan students usually practise one fixed technique at a time. In the long run, both aim to arrive at the same place.

The most common criticism of *kata* is that it generally does not allow *aiki* to develop; some train to produce perfect whole *kata* sets as their main aim, while others become entranced by technical detail. Perhaps the worst shortcoming of *kata* sequences as a learning approach is that a student can show good avoidance and *kuzushi*, great speed and dexterity in technique, yet lack *aiki* and never know it. Accordingly, once *aiki* is included, there is little problem with *kata*.

There are some perceptible advantages to studying *kata* sets. For example, repeating a certain *kata* many times enables the student to remember vast numbers of techniques. Often, the memory is collaborative. *Tori* may not remember in the moment, yet, when attacked by *uke* in a certain way, he knows exactly what to do – *tori* responds to the attack as trained, as his body remembers. Therefore, in *kata* it could be said that *uke* has the more demanding role as he has to remember what attacks to perform. As every technique often has a different attack, when the specific attack comes, a well-trained *tori* instinctively knows what to do – the technique just appears. This has obvious practical uses for self-defence. If someone attacks in like fashion, *tori* responds in exactly the same, trained way. Also, *kata* sets can be performed alone, without *uke*. In this way it is possible to run through multiple *kata*s and practise many techniques within a short time.

Just because O Sensei abandoned *kata* as a learning methodology does not mean that it should be dismissed lightly. It has to be remembered that O Sensei was a great martial artist and learned what he knew in *kata*-based approaches. He only discarded *kata* once he had absorbed the principles therein.

Static or Flowing

In static training, *uke* clamps on with a tight hold from a static position. Many schools use this method for beginners, yet it also remains important for seniors as it provides them with a link to basic movement. Once the basics are understood, *tori* initiates as, or even just before, *uke* grasps, resulting in continuity of flow, or *ki-no-nagare*. The most important point is to adhere to the principles of movement learned in the basics. If this is ignored, and there is no link between static and flow, then you are practising two separate arts that have little in common. The secret lies in combining the two.

Light and Heavy

Tori and *uke* can practise light or heavy, fast or slow. Light practice is good for co-ordination, heavy practice is good for technical skill; the two are indispensable for good *aiki* to develop. In *randori* or *jiyu-waza* practice, *uke* can vary the training, being light, responsive, firm or downright difficult. A happy medium to aim for is to be somewhere between responsive and firm, but it is imperative also to negotiate with *uke* and practise at either end of the spectrum.

Students should always try to create training situations that push or stress *tori* further. *Uke* should therefore make less obvious attacks, feint attacks, unusual attacks, and while receiving technique should offer various levels of resistance and additional counter-attacks; *uke* should not merely be an overly co-operative teddy bear for *tori* to play with. Most importantly, the sooner a freer aspect of training is realized the better. Sticking to standard forms for five years is not realistic. What is necessary is practice that promotes more movement and the means for *tori* to learn to compromise under different situations.

Naming the Attack or Naming the Technique

When training or grading, some schools of Aikido name the attack, some name the technique, some do both, few do none. Naming the attack means that you are necessarily concerned with dealing with a specific attack, and that it might be approached in several ways with several techniques or variations thereof, adding a degree of spontaneity. Naming the technique means that you must do a certain technique from a variety of attacks, testing the brain. Both these schools create speculative thought. Naming both the attack and the technique, however, robs the student of the opportunity to reflect in the moment. Naming neither is good for humiliation and often produces chaos at lower levels but is obviously the target to

Suwari-waza.

Hanmi handachi-waza.

aim for. The natural progression in a syllabus would be to name the attack and the technique, name the technique, name the attack, name neither.

Three Styles of Practice

Performing *suwari-waza* adds a completely new dimension to moving around for the average westerner. Once accustomed, *suwari-waza* isolates the legs somewhat from the postural equation and helps develop overall stability. Also noticeable is the fulcrum power generated by the knee just as it lowers to the floor. Of course, this is the point where it is useful to apply the technique and, to a less visible extent, it transfers unconsciously into your *tachi-waza*.

Hanmi-handachi techniques add another dimension and make you aware that, whether performing *suwari-waza* or *tachi-waza*, your feet should always be in such a position that it is possible to stand up or sit down quickly and comfortably.

Three Weapons

Producing all the techniques against the three weapons – the *tanto*, *bokken* and *jo* – potentially triples your repertoire at a stroke, and they can also be done from kneeling or half-standing positions. Practising many techniques against a single weapon provides the opportunity to discern strong and weak techniques – you have to be realistic and realize that some are far better than others. Also, practising a similar technique against different weapons allows you to get used to operating at different distances. It also shows how the tactics vary between weapons, both in terms of attack and defence.

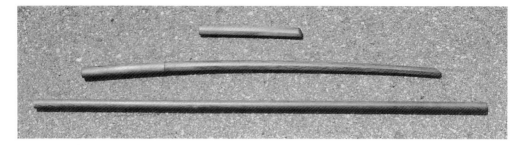

Tanto, bokken and *jo.*

Training to the Beat

Sometimes a class is just too slow. The teacher clacks two *tanto*s together, or, better, uses *keisaku*, two large pieces of hard wood that monks use for clapping: one clack means one technique, say, *shomen-uchi suwari-waza-ikkyo*. The teacher waits until everyone has finished – all students hold at the finish and wait. The teacher clacks again: for the first four times, students perform two *irimi* and two *tenkan*

Keisaku.

variations and the teacher waits until all the students have finished and the room is silent. *Tori* and *uke* do not change roles yet.

The teacher continues, but this time clacks when about half the class have finished. On hearing the clack, all techniques must stop, all *uke*s must rise and attack *tori*s immediately. The teacher continues for about ten more times, then *tori* and *uke* change roles and start again. After it is done, partners are changed, everyone moves on to the next technique, and it starts again. If on getting to *sankyo* or *yonkyo* some students do not know them, they should be encouraged to do *ikkyo* again. Finally, the class continues with a few *hanmi-handachi-waza* and *tachi-waza*. It is surprising how much can be got through in a short space of time with this kind of practice.

Another 'beat' training method is to follow the rhythm of music. This is particularly useful when training alone. The student repeats a certain movement on the left and right alternately for one complete rhythmic song. It is exhausting, and what is practised will infiltrate the sinews thoroughly, so it is important to be careful to perform only good technique.

Ninin-Dori

This two-on-to-one method of practice adds vigour to Aikido and can be further

144

developed with *sannin-dori* (three-on-to-one) or *tanin-dori* (multiple attack). Rather than being a test, this kind of practice should be used to develop skill. The practice can be varied in several simple ways and each time it is useful to concentrate on one aspect only:

- no attacks – *uke*s walk forward, *tori* evades;
- only one *uke* allowed to attack at a time, slowly;
- *tori* names the attack;
- the teacher names the attack;
- *uke*s choose one attack each then stick with that same attack;
- *uke*s all use striking attacks;
- *uke*s all use grabbing attacks;
- *tori* tries to do the same technique to different specified attacks;
- *tori* tries to do as many different techniques as possible from one method of attack;
- *uke*s and *tori* are free to do whatever they like. Obviously, this final example is the goal but a structured route will help tremendously.

Students in Aikido also practise escapes from *morote-dori* when held by two people. These techniques are not easy and force you to keep your centre while using both hands. Every teacher seems to have his own collection, but they are rarely shown, so the keen student must make sure to remember them if they are ever seen.

Renraku-Waza and *Kaeshi-Waza*

The practice of *renraku-waza* (combinations) and *kaeshi-waza* (reversals or counters) is an interesting method. Not often taught, *renraku-waza* link techniques together in logical progression. *Kaeshi-waza* are rarely done. Some say O Sensei taught

them to his senior students only. Obviously, such training is more common in a sporting style such as Judo. Further, Shodokan Aikido, the competitive style, has its very own *kaeshi-kata*.

One reason why *renraku-waza* are not generally taught might be because of the prevalent idea that the main technique is supposed to work; if it does not, the practitioner should figure it out rather than switching to an easier technique. There is some logic here, but it is wishful thinking to assume that one technique is always going to work. Accordingly, students should train with reality in mind and vary technique according to the situation.

Free Practice

Otherwise known as *randori* or *jiyu-waza*, free practice can mean anything from allowing the students a little time to do whatever they want to do, to plonking them in the middle of the mat and telling them to do *tanin-dori* against any attack. In Shodokan Aikido or Judo, *randori* is fighting. In traditional Aikido it is usually referred to as *jiyu-waza*, where *tori* is free to do anything.

Naturally, true free practice is excellent for the students. Typically, free practice is done towards the end of the class and students will practise what they have studied that day. At other times they can do whatever they like. In this way, *tori* and *uke* can negotiate their Aikido training rather than always have it dictated to them by the teacher.

Competition

After about three weeks of learning any style of traditional Aikido, the average beginner will no doubt begin to believe that competition is against Aikido principles. He will soon learn to support his stance with the argument that many Judo forms have disappeared since it entered the Olympics, or that sport Karate without *kata* has lost its essence. Yet, before starting Aikido, that same person probably enjoyed playing soccer or tennis, or some other competitive sport. The human mind can certainly be gullible and irrational.

Most Aikido students naturally have a competitive nature and bring it with them to the *dojo*. In the *dojo*, to a certain extent, the student is like the monk in the temple who tries to forget the external world. It is not easy, perhaps not even rational, but it is an important goal nevertheless. By not competing in Aikido, *aikidoka* have the chance to develop their ability to a higher level through co-operation. However, if the ultimate purpose – fighting – is ignored or forgotten, they may lose direction. In Aikido, the way practitioners test themselves is by making strong attacks when striking or grabbing and, at times, this can turn into a friendly kind of competition where *uke* tries to clobber *tori* or grab him so strongly that he cannot move.

When martial art becomes sport, the main problem is that the committed attack vanishes as both parties become overly cautious, in their desire not to be caught off guard or off-balance. Competition with form and rules complicates the art as it overly prescribes the method in which participants train. If competition is the way you want to go, you need a broader training programme that includes the traditional method and also covers every competition-illegal technique to be found; techniques are illegal in competition because they are dangerous, and they are dangerous because they work, but they can only be dangerous if you are good at them. If they are not practised because they are dangerous, then you are not practising a martial art – perhaps it could be called a

'martial sport'. So, in the case of, say, Shodokan Aikido, the competitive form of Aikido, whether it is sport or art can only be determined by how the participant trains, not by whether he enters competition.

Misogi

Some teachers hold a particularly gruelling class and call it *misogi*, or spiritual cleansing. Typically, the students do the same thing, for example, *shomen-uchi* with a *bokken*, for the whole lesson. Two things happen here: either your technique gets progressively worse, or it improves. The whole point of the ordeal is to develop the mental determination to continue in the face of adversity, overcoming fatigue and pain. In terms of technical development, however, there is a danger that it can have a detrimental effect on technique; it is when you are exhausted that what you really know comes out, or, worse, what you are doing really sinks in. If you are making bad technique, this will obviously be training a bad habit. If you can overcome the pain and continue to push out good technique then it will have a very positive effect, and you will be able to produce good technique under stress.

A more modern training method would dictate that you stop when the technique worsens, yet this would encourage many to give up too soon. The most useful benefit of *misogi* training in terms of technique is to move from the learned to the acquired, but it will only have a positive outcome if the technique is performed consistently well.

Play

Aikido can be great fun and it is not too difficult to invent interesting methods of practice. There are a number of interesting play ideas:

- From *shizen hontai*, partners push each other until one moves a foot, the object being not to move. This can be varied by taking it in turns to attack and defend, or having both attack together. More fun can be added by allowing pulling.
- Both partners walk towards each other along a line on the *tatami*, the object being to walk through each other. Obviously, one partner needs to be pushed off the line, allowing the other to continue straight ahead maintaining composure. Sometimes, both fall off the line. To make good practice, make it a rule that the forward walking movement cannot stop. This leads to a quick, dynamic decision.
- Make a Sumo ring with belts. With jackets on or off, push partners out of the ring, or make any part of their body touch the floor.
- Sit facing partners as in *suwari-waza kokyu-ho*. Simply, partners push each other over at the same time by any means whatsoever. Backwards can be dangerous if the person is not flexible. Pulling could also be allowed.
- Facing partners in a press-up position, try to knock your partner's arms away, making them fall down on their belly, or face if not careful.
- Have students put a *tanto* or a piece of paper in their belt at the rear. Students now have to run around and collect as many *tanto*s or papers as possible. This creates an almost battlefield-like situation and develops an idea of strategy.
- One game in Judo involves two people trying to steal each other's belts, standing, kneeling, or both. The wise teacher tells all the students to put their hands on their head while he explains the activity. This means they cannot suddenly tighten their belts! It is useful to make a rule that you may not deliberately touch your own belt.
- Two students run and clash into each other. *Uke* tries to maintain his post-clash position for a second or two, which gives *tori* the opportunity to recognize a shape to take advantage of to form into a technique.

With any game it is best to keep rules really simple and only make them more complicated once everyone has a clear understanding of what they are doing. The teacher's responsibility is to make sure it does not get too rough. The teacher has to create a sense of fun, but maintain control. Accordingly, it is not a good idea for the teacher to join in.

20 Strategy

In the field of observation, chance favours only the prepared mind. *Louis Pasteur*

To beat someone of another art, you need to know their art, but that is not to say that you should fight according to the ways of that art. In knowing your opponent's art, you will be aware of his strengths and avoid them; you will also be aware of his weaknesses and may utilize them. Accordingly, the wise do not display their art.

Zanshin

Hidden Zanshin

Keeping your *zanshin* hidden means that you are quietly alert, mindful of the aggressor but hiding your awareness inside; the antagonist remains unaware of what awaits. In this case, no direct threat is felt, so nothing needs to be done. Indeed, there are times when merely exposing your *zanshin* could lead directly to trouble.

Exposed Zanshin

If you choose to expose your *zanshin*, there is an obvious change in attitude. You confront the aggressor in terms of silence, words or action and he is aware of your presence. With silence, the way you look at a person shows him what you want to say; words make it clearer; action makes it happen. If you are aware of these processes, you can develop and use them to your advantage.

Fighting

Musashi advises that the spirit of fighting is fire. Keeping a cool mind in the face of an onslaught is easier said than done, but, if you are to be successful, it must be done. In order to practise overcoming hardship, the *aikidoka* obviously needs to find stressful situations and jump right in. The *dojo* exists to provide the means.

Learning

The average martial artist requires, more than a fighting strategy, a strategy of learning. There are numerous methods of practice, but what is really important is for the student to discern a principle from the experience. Without a principle, nothing has been learned. Teaching according to principles, it is possible to give seemingly different lessons every class. Taking one principle, the teacher should be able to show it through various media – empty-hand technique, *bokken* and *jo*. One principle does not mean one technique. One solid principle can be demonstrated across a range of different techniques. Often, a teacher may be doing exactly this without explaining, leaving it for the students to sort out in their own minds.

Ordinary technical-based teaching often confuses the students due to the seemingly endless range of techniques presented in no apparent logical order. After the students become accustomed to the idea of learning principles, however, they will be able to pick up seemingly new techniques, or shapes, instantly. The shape may be new, but the principle is old hat and learning becomes easy. The students have become true vehicles of transmission.

Self-Training

It is impossible to learn everything in the *dojo*. In order to make your art your own it is necessary both to think and to act. Thinking means analysing everything, sorting everything out and putting it all in order. This is especially important if you are to become a teacher. Acting means you have to act on what you have thought. You may write down your ideas on paper, but you really need to 'imprint' them in your sinews, muscles and bones. This can be done by repeatedly performing the techniques by yourself. With a partner no technique is the same, but when you are on your own you can make it the same, and get your body in order. Furthermore, you can run through multiple techniques or *kata* sets in a short space of time, covering and repeating them many times over.

In the beginning, simply go through the various forms, irrespective of the effect it might have on an imaginary *uke*. Next, 'see' the imaginary *uke* through the inner eye. Sometimes it may feel as though what is being done is wrong. Naturally, you need a good imagination; over time, this develops to the extent that the imaginary *uke* might even resist or change direction. Better still, you can imagine the real *uke* attacking a split second before he actually does so and be ready in advance.

Training in this way helps the student to understand Aikido much faster. Every Aikido technique can be practised like this and, on returning to the *dojo*, you will soon find that it translates into producing improved technique. Self-training can also be particularly useful in establishing links in movement between the empty-hand techniques and those of the *bokken* or *jo*. Once a common movement is determined, you can practise it with, say, the *bokken*, and the movement learned will easily transfer to the *jo* or back to the empty hand.

21 Self-Defence

A 'NO' uttered from deepest conviction is better and greater than a 'YES' merely uttered to please. *Mahatma Ghandi*

It is a point that is often forgotten or ignored, but most people who walk through the Aikido door are interested in learning self-defence.

Putting the Self First

Some say that the martial arts are a selfish pursuit. This might be true since, in survival, nothing comes before the self. For example, what should you do at the scene of a motor accident? First, it is necessary to slow down the other traffic, especially at night, otherwise there may be another collision, perhaps involving you. Next, if possible, you should call, or send someone to call, for an ambulance. Only then is it safe to attend to the victim(s). Clear thinking saves the day.

Another scenario might involve someone having difficulty in a river or pond. Here, the last thing you should do is to dive in and try to save them. Instead, you should stand at the edge and encourage the person to swim ashore, looking for a long stick or piece of cloth that can be extended out towards them. Failing that, you can get into the water, but you should not approach too near. In their desperation as they try to keep their head above water, people in danger of drowning often clamber on top of their rescuer; they are out of control and a serious threat to the rescuer's own safety. Entice them to swim towards you. If that has no effect and you

do decide to attempt a rescue, approach them from the rear, and be ready to slap them firmly if they get out of control. Your personal safety comes first. If they drown you, you will be unavailable to save them, or the next person. This principle is taught on life-saving courses, and is no doubt based on hard-earned experience. There are too many examples of people drowning needlessly while trying to save others. It may be 'heroic', but the death is often the result of misguided judgement.

Protecting Your Adversary

It is often said in Aikido that one should 'take care' of the attacker; the ideal of Aikido is *ai-nuke*, where both escape without injury. A nice philosophy, but just how is one to deal with a desperate attacker? The law says that one should initially give them what they want, but there undoubtedly comes a time when what they demand is too much (*see* Appendix III for the legal implications of using Aikido in self-defence). Rather than 'take care' of them, it makes more sense to say, 'spare them'. This implies that one has the ability to defeat them; one makes a conscious choice not to, and spares them. The underlying logic here, which is often misunderstood or not realized, is the realist view that one has to have the ability to destroy the antagonist, for without it, there can be no conscious choice to spare them. Such a resolute spirit is reflected in the Kenjutsu term *ai-uchi*, where both antagonists are killed by each other's swords simultaneously. What this means is that one's Aikido has to be martial in nature. If one's training spirit is resolute, one will not dally in daily life, nor quiver in a dangerous confrontation. One will be in control and thus will be able to let live, or let die. So, the more one wishes to help oneself or others, the leaner and meaner one's personal training needs to be. Anything less and it cannot be called a martial art.

Aikido for Practical Self-Defence

Aikido's best strategy for self-defence lies in analysing problematic situations and avoiding them before they worsen but, when push comes to shove, the way an individual has trained will determine the response. Those who train softly will respond softly; those who train hard will respond hard; those who have done both will have a choice. Whatever the style, proper training will ensure a good response – Aikido should work. If not, the problem lies with the school, or with the individual. In reality, however, even in a good school it takes much longer to become proficient in Aikido than in certain other arts.

As the vast majority of *aikidoka* spend their time training for co-ordination and harmony against overly co-operative *ukes*, it is worthwhile for the mid-level student to escape this and develop a separate repertoire of responses for self-defence. It may be that the student takes responsibility for his own learning, practising intensely by himself, or by studying other arts that cater more for self-defence. What the student will realize is that, while his *aiki* training experience may not yet have prepared him for practical self-defence, it will certainly have prepared him for learning the techniques of other arts much faster.

When practising for a self-defence scenario a compliant *uke* is not required, nor is clean technique. If the student has not yet risen to the level of being able to go with the flow, timing technique and *atemi* together in harmony, then he has little choice but to make the best out of bad technique, using all the dexterity he can muster; survival is more important than perfect technique. It ought to be part of a teacher's responsibility to expand his own Aikido by taking the principles of other arts on board so he can better prepare his students for self-defence. If practical applications of Aikido techniques or beyond are not done in class, the curious student will need to find them elsewhere.

It is useful to make a comparison of the different methods.

1. Pure Aikido: if the technique does not work you have to figure out why. It includes strong attacks with some *atemi* in the techniques. The aim is to produce clean techniques in perfect harmony with the attack.
2. Practical Aikido: if the technique does not work, it needs to be changed to something that will. Less harmony is acceptable and the emphasis is on taking control and making it work. Over time, such technique may become more efficient, moving towards pure Aikido.
3. Self-defence: rough and ready, the technique has to work no matter what. Survival today is more important than perfection in technique tomorrow. Of course, progressing through the years, the rough-and-ready style becomes more efficient and controlled, yet remains hard and brutal in essence.

The legal implications of using Aikido for self-defence are discussed in Appendix III.

22 The Syllabus and Grading

It's better to be looked over than it is to be overlooked.
Mae West

Most martial arts syllabuses are a mish-mash of spurious techniques. To beginners in Aikido the syllabus is quite unfathomable. At best, by the time they reach *Shodan* they might understand; at worst, they may still have no clue where they stand. Often, they cannot see what they do know, nor can they see what they need to know, let alone figure it out. Obviously, for beginners or intermediates, the situation will be more acute.

Logical Progress

A good syllabus ought to be clear and logical. For example, for beginners or intermediates, it could start with eight attacks and ten basic techniques, making a total of eighty when combined. In natural progression, the attacks might typically be the following:

1. *ai-hanmi katate-dori*;
2. *gyaku-hanmi katate-dori*;
3. *sode-dori*;
4. *mune-dori*;
5. *shomen-uchi*;
6. *yokomen-uchi*;
7. *tsuki*;
8. *ushiro ryote-dori*.

The techniques might be the following:

1. *ikkyo*;
2. *nikyo*;
3. *sankyo*;
4. *yonkyo*;
5. *gokyo*;
6. *irimi-nage*;
7. *kote-gaeshi*;
8. *shiho-nage*;
9. *kaiten-nage*;
10. *tenchi-nage*.

The first part of this mini-syllabus is to practise one technique a week from eight attacks. Practising from all eight attacks each lesson keeps the single technique interesting and shows students the extent of what they need to know. Although it may be confusing at first, by the end of the week it will begin to make sense. Part two of the mini-syllabus is based on the attack. This time, all ten basic techniques are practised every lesson against a single attack. This is best modified by the addition of two *kokyu-nage* techniques, *irimi* and *tenkan*, performed at the beginning of the lesson, and carefully chosen to provide a basis in common movement and principle between the techniques to be done that day. Accordingly, if you are doing an *ai-hanmi katate-dori* attack, the way the *kokyu-nage* is taught should dictate the method by which each and every one of the ten basic techniques is performed.

Part one is a mechanical introduction, while part two allows students to get a feel for similarities, or the common principles that bind Aikido together. Obviously, it takes ten weeks to work through part one, and eight weeks to finish part two of this mini-syllabus. Adding a week of revision at the end of each part would make a total of twenty weeks, after which time the students would have had a significant amount of basic practice. Keen beginners would be able to claim to know eighty techniques fairly well. They would probably remember what they know and be able to perform on demand if asked. Any gaps in their knowledge would be readily apparent to other beginners watching. Finally, if they are shown a few more attacks or techniques, what has to be done is already known – they will be able to figure out and fill in unknown gaps. Better still, such logical knowledge cannot easily be forgotten.

A logical syllabus should ensure that students cover the whole range of techniques in a finite period. It can be repeated at will or used to attract newcomers. A logical syllabus contributes to attendance since it compels students to train – if they miss a week, they miss a segment of their learning. It contributes to learning because students can help each other fill in the gaps if something is missed. It contributes to common sense because it places the tools of learning in the hands of the students.

Many a school has a random approach to teaching. At best, it serves to stimulate the students to thought as the teacher hands out doses of interesting principles. At worst, there is no structure or logic and the result is boring training with no perceivable direction towards progress.

Weapons Syllabus

Some students receive weapons grades in Aikido. The problem here is that the weapons of Aikido are not an end in themselves, but a means to improve your Aikido. The weapon system in Aikido cannot compete with arts such as Kenjutsu, Jodo, Escrima or Silat, which concentrate exclusively on weapons. *Aiki-ken* is not Kenjutsu and so should not be compared with it. It may be that, the closer to real Kenjutsu the *Aiki-ken* is, the better the training can be, but *Aiki-ken* exercises are none the less designed first and foremost to help your Aikido.

One practical idea for weapons-related gradings might be for them to be self-awarded, as follows: if students all wore protective clothing and battered each other to hell, a 'self-grading' could be achieved by those who were prepared to remove some of that clothing, thereby making the statement that they were good enough not to get hit, or tough enough not to mind.

Losing Direction

Most of those who start Aikido ultimately quit, even *yudansha*. There are many reasons and one of them is that they find the syllabus boring. The fault here is usually that the student has been driven by the syllabus and that, when getting up to third or second *kyu* or so, it all begins to look pretty much the same – there are few, if any, new techniques to learn. Students fail to realize that in Aikido there are simply fewer basic techniques than in other arts. They must come to terms with the fact that progressing in Aikido does not mean learning innumerable new moves; it means performing the original ones better.

You can only really begin to learn Aikido once you have fallen in love with the basics and this shows in your development more than you might realize. The source of advanced techniques is found in the basics and, once this is realized, advanced gradings actually become rather meaningless. Those students who always have an eye on the next grade are the ones who ultimately fail really to learn and who end up quitting. Inevitably, their foolishness catches up with them one day, as they realize that they may have the grade, while they lack the requisite skill.

Grading

The belted grading system is relatively new, stemming from Kano Jigoro's modernized Judo, and has been adopted by most Japanese, Korean and even Chinese arts. However, many Aikido schools use only white and black belts with *yudansha* wearing *hakama*, which somehow gives the art its own special niche.

The syllabus itself is good for the students because their training appears to be organized. The actual test is useful in that it provides focus and forces the students to demonstrate their skill under duress. The very first grading and the *Shodan* grading are very important events – both loom omnipresent during training. If your first grading is done well, all the subsequent ones will be easy. It is better to wait and get it right than to rush in early and look foolish. If you train well and perform the first test well, future tests will probably be much easier.

Preparation

For gradings, students obviously need to learn the techniques on the grading syllabus. The problem here is that some clubs practise nothing but the grading syllabus. They pair off people of a similar grade and do nothing but what is required for the next grading; that is their total training experience. It is easy to teach, of course, and allows students to advance rapidly up the grading ladder, but a more natural approach is better.

In a more natural approach, everyone trains together and everyone changes partners every time the technique changes, or every time the students sit down and receive further explanation. Over a period of several months any beginner ought to have experienced all of the basic techniques and should discover to his delight that he has covered most, if not all and more, of what he needs to do for his next grading. If he is unsure of anything on the syllabus, he can then ask any senior or the teacher for advice.

Practice for a grading ought be no more than a week in advance, and even that might be too much; if you have to train for a grading it means you are not ready for it. This approach places responsibility for grading firmly upon the shoulders of the students. It encourages them to seek, rather than have the teacher show. The teacher becomes a guide. Before gradings, you sometimes see pairs of curious students trying to figure out new techniques they have not yet been taught by following principles they have acquired in other techniques. The power of curiosity!

Purpose

The main advantage of grading is to provide the student with a stressful situation to be overcome. Those under stress often resort to their crudest form of technique; the grading makes the students aware of this, both in their own performance and in the observation of others, and proper training will correct it. In Japan, a teacher almost always knows and grades his own students, but this was not possible for years in the West because of a lack of senior instructors. As a result, grading was done in front of people who barely know the student. Many teachers have bureaucratic standards written in triplicate and set in stone that have to be met in order to pass the grading. (Some even pass all the students to rake in the money.) There is another method, although it is nowadays not common, in which grading is seen as a recognition of improvement. After some time, the teacher who per-ceives a notice-able improvement will simply grade a student on the spot.

Growth

Anyone who has trained for a while will know that the initial learning curve is steep but then levels off, reaching a plateau. Some people stay on their plateau for what seems like an age and then, one day, something happens and they realize they have jumped up a notch. This is equivalent to a grading, except that it is the self, instead of the teacher, who discerns a radical improvement. If the teacher discerns it, it could also be interpreted that the student has just jumped up a notch, whether a grade has been awarded or not. Here, what is recognized is a noticeable improvement in skill. This is very different from just learning a new set of techniques and demonstrating them in mediocre fashion to pass the next grading.

People improve in different ways. Some overcome repressive fear, some overcome a physical disability, some lose a lot of weight, some become more positive in outlook, some suddenly become more co-ordinated, and so on. The struggle is different in every case, and an outside teacher coming in for a day to grade can know little of every personal experience. In this sense, it certainly seems unlikely that a group of people could be ready for grading at the same time.

Feedback

Feedback on gradings can be counter-productive. While it might help a student to correct his weaknesses, students need to be given every reason to think, so that they can educate themselves. Far more progress will be made if they have to figure out where their own problems lie and form their own solutions. If the student cannot figure it out, then more training may be in order. The more explanation he is given, the less chance the student has of figuring things out for himself and having his own mini-enlightenment – which is the whole point of self-development in any sphere.

Encouragement or Criticism

It seems that there is a modern, perhaps Western, trend in study or recreation to encourage the learner, and tell him how well he did even if he was hopeless. There is no doubt that this aids the learning process. This thinking also exists in modern sports and, recently, extends to martial arts. It may be useful, but in martial arts there should be little or no praise. Clapping in praise is also inappropriate. Whether a martial artist does well or does badly should be of no concern to the onlooker. It is a personal quest. He should not need to be praised by others; if he does need it, he needs to get rid of that need.

If praise is to be given it should be sparingly, and only to those of low ability in desperate need of a boost. Martial artists need constant criticism, and they need to learn to respond positively to that criticism and not take it personally. It goes without saying that the criticism should be honest and not overdone. The army sergeant may shout like crazy at the recruit who cannot get over the wall, but once he is over, nothing more is said – not being able to get over is death, getting over is life. The sergeant puts up barriers for the soldier to overcome. The teacher criticizes to push the students to examine themselves.

If a student performs a series of techniques poorly, he may rightly doubt his skill. If he is applauded (which often happens), he may become elated, as though he has just done exceedingly well. Worse, he might become conceited, actually believing the praise. This is ridiculous. All that is necessary is honesty. In fact, whether it was good or bad, nothing need be said. It is a personal journey. If what was shown was of little skill, or of great skill, it is of no consequence – it only shows the level the student is at, and his stage along the Way. Criticism exists everywhere and being exposed to it in the *dojo* gives the student the chance to train himself mentally to deal with it in ordinary life. Perhaps those teachers whom you can never please are the best teachers.

23 Other Arts

I don't like that man. I must get to know him better.
Abraham Lincoln

People often wonder why O Sensei decided to include particular techniques in Aikido. Certainly, his experience was broad and his Aikido never remained static. Did he tire of traditional *kata*-based teaching and switch to an *aiki*-centred one? Did he have a fixed syllabus in mind at each stage of development? Or did it just evolve, as techniques were added, or devolve, as superfluous movements were excluded? Did he catch the peace bug after Japan's loss in the War? Was he somehow freed to go his own way after the death of his mentor, Takeda Sokaku? This curiosity is no doubt felt by many and fuels their quest in studying O Sensei and the arts he studied, most notably, Daito-ryu aiki-jujutsu.

Searching for the Source
In the past, few *aikidoka* considered Daito-ryu aiki-jujutsu in relation to Aikido. In more modern times, the revival of ancient Jujutsu arts owes much to interested foreigners, many of whom have been curious as to the roots of Aikido or Judo. Some have come to believe that what they lack, even after years of training, can be found in the more traditional arts. It is good that they search, but unfortunate that what they discover might not increase their chances of finding what they seek. This is because they expect to be taught, yet what they seek may come only from within.

For Ueshiba, Aikido was progressive, he changed it as time moved on and, as such, his Aikido 'developed'. The strongest point of Daito-ryu aiki-jujutsu, as a traditional art, is that it is static; it preserves the ancient techniques in the form of unchanging *kata*. In the traditional school, everything is transmitted from the all-knowing master. However, while Aikido is progressive, it nevertheless has very strong foundations. For example, some learn it in Europe, others in the USA, yet when they meet they find themselves to be doing almost exactly the same thing. That is remarkable for a progressive art and just shows how non-progressive in essence *aiki* principles must be. In a learning environment, an approach that places responsibility for learning in the hands of the keen, thinking student stands a better chance of transmission in the long run.

If you learn and discover, you are more likely to understand the essence and be able to pass it on. To the credit of the art, many Aikido *dojo*s have an element of freedom that allows students to rediscover for themselves. But this is not a criticism of Daito-ryu aiki-jujutsu. When considering the 'old', it is vital to be aware of the immense human inventiveness that went into the discovery. The best minds of old were no less than the best of today – it is just that the world looks a little different now. Anyway, looking for the roots of

Aikido in Daito-ryu aiki-jujutsu is not useful, since the two are of a different age. For the roots of modern Aikido, practitioners ought look into Ueshiba the man; while his main background may have been Daito-ryu aiki-jujutsu, in the post-war years he rejected set *kata* as a teaching methodology and went his own way.

Aikido Styles

Judo, Karate and Aikido are all quite different arts with separate histories, having no apparent connections. It is almost as though the heads of each school got together, decided their particular territories, and determined that they would not trespass; indeed, this has even been said. There are several schools of Judo and Karate, and Aikido is no different, but analysing the differences in Aikido styles is of little use; it is the similarities that make them all Aikido. For example, *aiki* – a fluid feeling that exists between two practitioners – can be found in many arts, not only Aikido. However, it is Aikido that names it and practises it; no matter what the style of Aikido, all aim to develop an *aiki* feeling.

Style is no different from tradition – some people do it one way, others another. The defining essence of a style is usually found in its head teacher – it is personal – and to some extent all develop a cult of personality. Even within a style, each individual teacher will have his own idiosyncrasies that give definition to his club. Some of these differences are apparent in capability, personality and purpose. Teachers will always tend to concentrate on what they do best and thus their capabilities define their form. For example, flexible teachers will include many stretching exercises. An athletic teacher will have a vigorous warm-up. Shorter teachers might incorporate more hip throws. A teacher's personality will also be reflected in his teaching; some may be meek and polite in nature, while others may bellow and pound their *uke*s into the *tatami*.

The reason why a student trains could be anything ranging from boredom to a need for fitness, stress reduction, weight reduction or increased self-confidence, or a desire to learn self-defence. The teacher's bias will give direction but it may be moulded somewhat by the students' perceived needs and the local environment. All these differences add up to one teacher being slow and meticulous and another fast and furious. This can be the case even when both teachers have studied under the same teacher themselves.

Comparison with Other Arts

Who would win, a table tennis player or a tennis player? And what if they play with a shuttlecock instead of a ball? And who would win if they played badminton instead? It is not a good idea to worry too much about comparisons. *Aikidoka* should concentrate on developing the self and the method of choice is vigorous martial training. There are many martial arts and some are more rigorous or realistic than others. In sport, participants train to win and the path is narrowed by rules. In Budo the path is broad, encompassing the whole experience of life and death. The one who survives the day is the one who trains in the most appropriate way. Today, in my country, there is no war, so I train accordingly. If war is imminent, I will train accordingly. If war is upon me, I will act accordingly.

Visiting Other *Aiki* Arts

The first thing many students encounter when visiting or joining another style of *aiki dojo* is resistance. What seems to happen is that a new student is viewed with suspicion, the seniors try to resist and only allow the technique to work if it is done their way. Different *dojo*s, sometimes even within the same organization, seem to go through this same routine. The obvious question is whether your techniques really work at all. The answer is that you have to make them work and such a path is far from easy. This process of humiliation and false enlightenment needs to be experienced and overcome.

Studying Other Arts

People study additional arts because they find something lacking in their own or find something interesting elsewhere. As Aikido does not place emphasis on kicking or punching, it is only natural that the curious mind seeks the answer in another place. People seem to make two kinds of choices. The majority seem to choose an additional art that adds something new yet at the same time offers to improve their overall ability. These people might choose Judo to improve their throwing skills, Kenjutsu to improve their sword skills, or Taichichuan to improve their balance or develop their *Chi*, or *Ki*. Others might choose something completely different such as Karate, or Kung-fu. Choosing to study a mixture of these arts may, at first, come from simple curiosity. Later, it may be the result of a desire to improve your Aikido.

If you do choose to go down this road, it is important to keep the arts separate. You cannot enter the Aikido *dojo* and use a Kung-fu stance. If you have learned to box, you should not chide fellow *aikidoka* with the dumb 'What would you do if...' type of question. If they want to know, they have to ask it to themselves. If you have practised other arts it may be that you have asked yourself this very question and have done something about finding the answer.

After much training, most students come to realize that there are many inconsistencies between movements in the different arts, necessitating a decision – should you give up a certain art completely, or modify what you do within your preferred art for yourself? If you do the latter, and come to teach a particular art, you should teach it as it was taught, not with your personal modifications, otherwise the tradition will be lost and the students will be confused. Your own personal methods are based upon your own personal experience. Rather than teaching a certain 'move' from, say, Jujutsu, it might be better to encourage students to take classes in Jujutsu, just as you did. Alternatively, if you are capable, give a whole class in it from time to time, to let the students know about it.

Variety can add spice to life and you need to identify in the other arts the principles that match those of Aikido, and make them your own. It is the similarities that determine the strength of the principles, not the differences, which could sometimes be interpreted as being mistakes.

Giving a Class to Non-*Aikidoka* Martial Artists

If you are called upon to give a class to non-*aikidoka* martial artists, devise a lesson plan that shows the totality of Aikido, to make sure they get the whole picture:

• start with a couple of simple *kokyu-nage* covering the concepts of *irimi* and *tenkan*;
• show most or all of the basic techniques;
• if possible, do each one from a different attack;
• explain how each of them can be done from each attack, perhaps giving a short demonstration;

- do *kokyu-nage* again and explain how the method of training can be used as a bridge to make the techniques more effective;
- at the end, allow the students to ask questions, and answer honestly.

If you go in with the one-technique-per-lesson approach, you need not expect a second invitation. It will be impossible to teach anything properly in just one session, so your aim should be instead to give a brief insight into a more total picture of Aikido, which might spark natural interest. Even if it does not, at least they will be better informed.

Caution must also be taken when approaching students of more competitive arts, as they will naturally be keen to test your mettle. Starting with *suwari-waza* techniques may give you the advantage, as they are likely to encounter difficulty. If answers to questions are lacking then doubt is created and the whole process is wasted effort. Students with good etiquette may still show respect, but the seeds of doubt will be sown nevertheless.

Giving a Demonstration

Spectators view demonstrations as entertainment and Aikido demonstrations are usually awful in that respect. Worse, they are often placed amidst demonstrations of other arts that audiences find far more appealing because of their violent aspects. Any demonstration of Aikido ought, none the less, to provide an audience with a true idea of what Aikido is. Equal emphasis should be given to the more 'boring' aspects of the art, such as etiquette. Such attention to detail can spark the interest of the right kind of person, a parent who wants to instil some discipline in a teenage son, for example. Techniques look pretty much all the same to the average spectator so a slower methodological demonstration, coupled with an explanation, will better inform the more intelligent spectator about the true nature of Aikido. It will also show that you know what you are talking about.

You can make the finish more dynamic in nature, but not overly so. Keep it simple. Sword taking, suspect at best, ought be kept away from demonstrations. Likewise, throwing five *uke*s on top of each other is fun in the *dojo* but can look ridiculous in a demonstration to eye of the critical spectator. The simplest guideline is never to show what you cannot do well.

24 Philosophy

The man who views the world at 50 the same as he did at 20 has wasted 30 years of his life. *Muhammad Ali*

War has been man's eternal task and he rationalizes it to himself with philosophy. Some philosophy is created by leaders to encourage men to fight. More philosophy is created by men to make sense of the chaos in which they find themselves. Other philosophy is created by those who have survived to make sense of what happened. The type of philosophy that appeals to man is likely to be determined by where he is in time and his proximity to death.

Takemusu

The point at which a student's training has reached a particular level so that martial techniques appear, or are 'born' spontaneously when attacked, is known as *takemusu*. This term literally means 'birth of martial' and is commonly seen written in scrolls hanging in Aikido *dojo*s. With these scrolls, *aikidoka* like to remind themselves that they are training to develop a sense of martial awareness. Since we stopped stealing caves from bears and sabre-tooth tigers to live in, we have slowly forgotten what every wild animal on the planet knows – life is a ceaseless struggle for survival. Animals have various capabilities: speed, strength, stealth, cunning, poison, claws and teeth. Each animal has its place and lives according to its own strengths and weaknesses. In any garden, below the grass, in the trees, there exists a constant battle. The squirrel, for example, is either still, or fast-moving; it does not have the peace of day to walk. When still, it is alert, ceaselessly on the lookout for predators. If there are none, it darts a short distance then checks again – the squirrel that fails to maintain this lookout is eaten.

In comparison, having no predators, man is asleep. Outside of his cosy home, alertness for him is more occasional; it means taking care when crossing a road or anticipating hazards when driving. Inside, it may be apparent when dealing with his parent, teacher, boss or wife. More personally it is reflected in what he eats and drinks and the way he takes care of his health. It goes without saying that some are better practised than others, but in ordinary daily life there is often little to raise the adrenalin in the martial sense. Moreover, while training in a martial art may bring the participant a little closer to that level of 'animal awareness', no one will ever truly reach it – nor would a sane person want to. Looking for trouble in order to come to terms with it is not a sensible choice; seeking danger to test yourself is likely to see you quickly removed from the gene pool. The point to make is that Aikido is a martial art whose purpose is survival – let the battle begin!

Religion

O Sensei was a religious man but never required the same from his students. Many people are lost, looking for a way to go, and they should be allowed to find their own way. If a teacher regards himself as some enlightened guru, every aspect of his life will be scrutinized by his students, who will, no doubt, find many faults. There have been many wise men in human history and wise is he who reads them all; stupid is he who follows but one.

In the past, a person's religion dictated the way he lived. Nothing could be questioned because nothing else was known; the unruly ones had to bend their will to fit the teachings. Now, the world has become a cultural soup; people shop for religion until they find what meets their needs, and, if it later proves disagreeable, it is discarded for a more suitable one. Some even try to force it upon others. Most students approach Aikido to learn self-defence; few are interested in their teacher's personal philosophy, and even fewer are interested in adopting it for themselves. Teachers who demand such adherence are heading towards the beginnings of a cult – let the student beware!

World Peace

The Communists stated that they desired world peace and many were taken along for the ride. If they had read the small print, however, they would have realized that their quest for world peace was dependent upon conquering the world at the point of a gun. Some Aikido and Daito-ryu teachers waffle on about love and peace. There is nothing wrong in this, of course, but where are they coming from? Does anyone seriously think that such ideas had anything to do with approaching the skill of, say, Takeda Sokaku?

Before the Second World War, Japan was the leading military power in the East and its methods were brutal. Incredibly, when the Emperor declared an end to the War

his soldiers put down their guns and went home. The Japanese age of peace began and an anti-war constitution was adopted. General McArthur, that last Shogun of Japan, outlawed all martial arts and from this time on, martial artists began to emphasize peace talk. The almost immediate shift from war and death to peace and life throughout the nation is highly commendable but in terms of martial arts and martial training it is difficult to equate the two. All the great post-war masters had their origins in pre-war training regimens. The over-indulgence in peace chatter in modern martial arts is perhaps used more as a justification excuse for practising what are obviously deadly arts. Surely, martial artists need to be more honest about the origins of what they are doing.

Morals

Although each country has its laws, not all people are in agreement. While each religion has its faith, not all adherents follow. Most have their morals yet none have the same. Law, faith and morals combine to make the societal man; at their worst they confuse, and result in conflict. What is right for one person may be wrong for another; human beings all stand at some point along a very broad continuum. Some compete, others are quiet. Who is to say which way is best? All too often, those who are strong persuade and lead, while those who are meek listen and follow. The only way forward is to find your own path out of the mire.

Wisdom

Wisdom can be apparent in many forms. The Ancient Greeks would say that knowledge is a kind of wisdom. With correct knowledge, it is possible to determine the right decision. Courage is a kind of wisdom and is often required to make the

Meeting of cultures.

right decision. Perseverance is a kind of wisdom and is often required to carry out that decision to completion. What is apparent here is that wisdom is more than just knowledge; it is a more total life experience. It is not possible to pass this wisdom from one man to the next; it comes from within.

Ideals

Ideals need to be set and maintained by conscious effort to allow humans to rise above the level of animals. Roman civilization was built on ideals such as the state, city, society and the citizen. Its decline was a result of a decay in the Romans' belief in their own ideals and its ultimate destruction was orchestrated by those who had none; mankind was plunged into the Dark Ages. Today, everyone lives within the standards set by society yet such cultural norms are not visible, and are therefore rarely considered. In order to reach a

higher level, you need to become aware of ideals by which to live. If you cannot recognize and live up to a standard set by yourself, it will be impossible to conform to those set by others in society.

Martial Culture

All martial arts have their own particular cultures that broadly represent the values and mores of the particular society at large. Strip away the human element and all that is left is fighting, and if what remains is different from that of another culture then there may be a problem with that fighting system. Give all men clubs, knives and swords, and send them off to battle; the survivors will develop much the same methods and stratagems: avoid strike, poke sharp end into heart, whack man on head with club, enemy is dead. If a particular culture dictated that participants should bow before battle, a fighter of another culture would take the opportunity

163

to remove his opponent's head. If another offered a hand to be shaken, it would be chopped off. In this sense, culture, the very thing that makes men social beings, is martial weakness. You need to bear in mind that the essence of fighting is just that, and nothing else. It is all very well to train for the essence, but you also need to develop the mind so that you never need to use it.

Health

It is not easy to prevent the wanton destruction of the living environment. As an individual, the most you can do is not add to it; by living healthily and wisely, you should not become a burden on society. These days, many people reach middle age all the while drinking, smoking and overeating, and taking part in barely any physical exercise. The closest they will ever get to flowing is if they drown in a river; the closest they will ever get to harmonizing with nature is when they are six feet under – and then they turn up at the *dojo* door. Starting a martial art in such a condition is likely to add to their destruction; it would be better to send them elsewhere.

Regular training in Aikido develops and maintains flexibility and stamina. The body strengthens naturally and becomes somewhat resistant to injury and pain. The stronger the body is, the better it survives the shock and trauma of physical training. While injuries threaten, good health ensures that they heal faster, yet discipline and a keen sense of attention serve to keep them at bay. One thing to beware of is that the fitness developed over several years can disappear within a relatively short period of inactivity.

The first few months of Aikido training are often accompanied by muscle aches and pains in all sorts of places. Bruising is common, and more so in the unfit. Knocks, twists and sprains occur occasionally, but, despite the number of joint-related techniques in Aikido, torn ligaments, fractures, dislocations or broken bones are far less frequent. The most common causes of injury are bad break-falls, or crashing into and falling on top of each other. Sudden movement as the result of shock or surprise can cause muscle or tendon injury. A badly lain *tatami* can trap the toes. When training near the edge of the *tatami*, *uke* might hit the wall, or, stepping over the edge of the *tatami*, he might sprain an ankle. Too much sweat on the *tatami* can cause people to slip.

It is a particular trait in Aikido that injured persons tend to continue training, although, of course, this is done more carefully. A sprained ankle or twisted shoulder, for example, provides an opportunity to the student to refine his break-fall to a greater degree of perfection. Other injured students often turn up to training to watch. Sometimes, it is the case that careful training when injured actually aids the healing process, albeit under the careful advice of a doctor.

A martial arts teacher has a lot of influence. By not smoking or drinking, being unfit or grossly overweight, he sends an obvious message to his students, who may respond likewise without a word being spoken. That being said, there is nothing wrong with speaking your mind. If the government can tell us that smoking, drinking and being overweight are bad for the health, then a teacher can say so too. The craft is in not being outright rude in front of others. Accordingly, if your teacher tells you something that you do not like to hear, get used to it, respond to it, overcome it.

Sport

For O Sensei, Aikido was a martial art, not a sport. It was Tomiki Kenji who created sport Aikido. The former school of thought dictates that you must be better today than you were yesterday; the latter states that you should be better than your peers. As in any debate, where you sit is where you stand but simple observation will show that the greatest athletes of today are the greatest they have ever been in history and this is because of competitive sport. Certain individual key sports, such as archery, discus and javelin, reflect the fact that sport has long been the means through which warriors of old were trained. Furthermore, the Olympic Games have for a century provided the means through which states have competed, at times almost as though at war, yet thankfully instead of it.

In a martial art the problem posed by the sport element is the existence of restrictive rules. Most rules are for safety, and what is effective is often not allowed. It is strange, then, that Tomiki's rules contrast exactly with those of Judo, since what is allowed in one is not allowed in the other. Here, it seems the rules are defining styles, not danger. Another interesting point is that traditional Aikido extends its non-competitiveness to the personality suggesting that it is wrong to have a competitive nature. Surely any general in military history would want his soldiers to be competitive? The fact is that traditional Aikido has no competition and evangelizes non-competitive ideals, but to disregard it outright makes no sense. When you walk out of the *dojo* you enter into a world of competition. Are you prepared?

Making Money
There is nothing wrong with making money teaching martial arts. Any problem usually lies in the way the *dojo* is run. Simply, some teachers get lazy, stop teaching regularly, and pass on their duties to senior students. Often, the teacher might make a special appearance teaching secret techniques and in the worst case will demand extra course fees. As the situation worsens, such teachers may proclaim enlightenment, begin wearing strange clothes, teach yoga, prescribe healing remedies, offer courses on massage and meditation, and preach anything exotic – all in an attempt to extract more money. This is the surest way to nowhere. Students will feel they are not getting what they are paying for and will, invariably, leave. However, some find such 'gurus' appealing, following their self-made masters everywhere, being at their constant beck and call, eager to please in the vain hope of receiving recognition. Some *dojo*s develop cult-like characteristics, with money as their sole, yet denied, *raison d'être*. Avoid them.

If a teacher cannot teach all the time himself, paying other instructors a decent stipend will make the school more professional in nature. Making a clear timetable of who is teaching what and when will give the students the idea that the *dojo* is being run properly.

Social Aspects
Aikidoka are generally quite sociable. From the laying of the *tatami* through after-training tea or going out together socially, Aikido offers its practitioners multiple opportunities to talk and reflect on training. It is often here, in discussion, that the student learns far more about Aikido.

25 Conclusion

This is not the end. It is not even the beginning of the end. But it is, perhaps, the end of the beginning. *Winston Churchill*

Even if you are one of those who has come to believe that all life is insignificant, while here, it certainly makes sense to make the most of it.

Effective Training

The warm-up is vigorous, as the body should be ready both for class and for life. The exercises done are all related to forming good *aiki* habits, not merely to strength conditioning. Bowing to partners is done once before, and once after each change in partners – any more is wasted energy. *Ukemi* must be taken both very softly and very hard according to the student's ability, remaining responsive at all times. Harder *ukemi* and stronger attacks should always be striven for, not avoided. *Zanshin* should be present from the beginning of the class to the end, not just at the end of each technique, and should reveal itself in form through the posture, and in spirit though the mind via the eyes. Of course, if it continues outside the *dojo*, so much the better.

Breathing must continue throughout the technique, for both *tori* and *uke* are alive. *Kiai* can be loud or silent; the loud is for concentrated technique – power; the silent exists in the mind within a concentrated breath – harmony. Therefore, *kiai* when practising by oneself, not with a partner.

Shapes are preferred to names: *irimi-nage* shape, *ikkyo* shape, and so on. More often than not, a name sets an otherwise variable technique in stone. *Kokyu-ho* and *kokyu-nage* should have no predetermined form, just principle. Seek the principles, not the form, and try to apply them in technique. Different techniques should have more in common than differences and those commonalities are the key. The typical grading syllabus is often an incomplete, limited assortment of techniques – it should not be the main guide for learning.

Effective Study

To come to terms with the apparent mass of technical information in Aikido it is necessary for the learner to gather all the parts, analyse them, and sort and place them into a sensible framework. Everyone's experience is different and so each student's framework will vary. Once a framework is being built, everything will slowly begin to fall into its natural place. Certain things may not fit and might even be discarded. Accordingly, you will know what you know and will be ready to impart it to others.

Effective Purpose

Whether Aikido works or not depends upon the individual. For many, Aikido only exists while being practised, in much the same way as, say, table tennis. However, if you can maintain a level of awareness outside of the *dojo*, it can be said that your *aiki* is working. Awareness can be reflected in your posture, breathing, *ki* extension, and sense of danger. If you have developed *aiki*, if you have become healthier, if you have become calmer in nature, if you have become more aware of your body, if you have become more confident, if you have become more aware of danger, if you have avoided a potential problem, then your *aiki* has already worked and may, indeed, still be working. Of course, if you took that mugger's wallet from him and sent him on his way, your *aiki* could also be said to have worked.

There is no end.

Appendix I: Technical Drawings from *Shomen-Uchi*

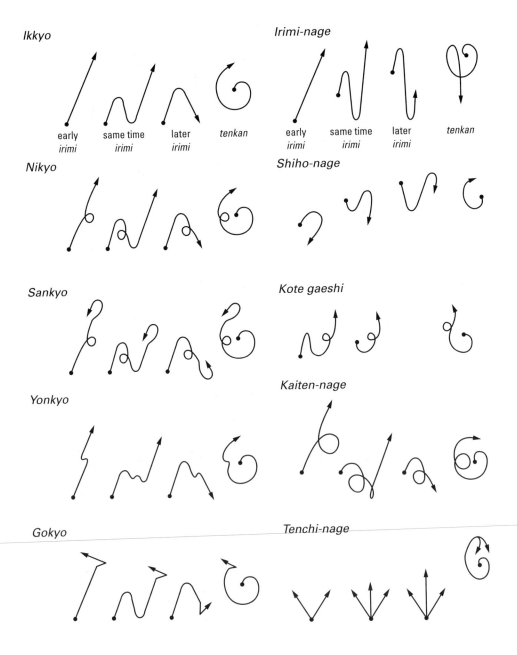

Ikkyo

early irimi   same time irimi   later irimi   tenkan

Irimi-nage

early irimi   same time irimi   later irimi   tenkan

Nikyo

Shiho-nage

Sankyo

Kote gaeshi

Yonkyo

Kaiten-nage

Gokyo

Tenchi-nage

Appendix II: Technical Drawings from *Yokomen-Uchi*

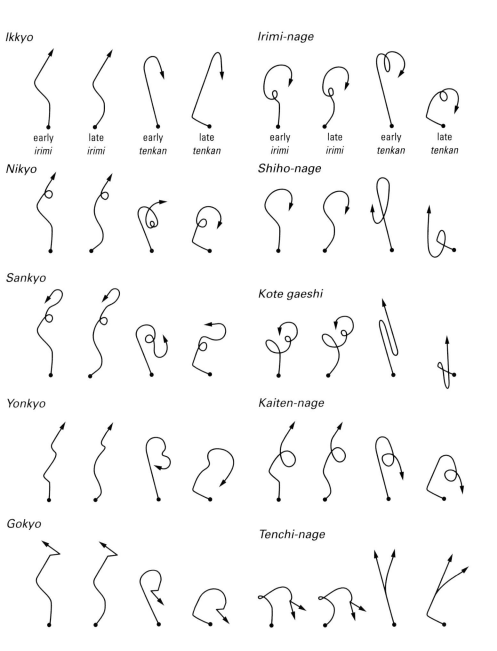

Ikkyo — early irimi, late irimi, early tenkan, late tenkan

Irimi-nage — early irimi, late irimi, early tenkan, late tenkan

Nikyo

Shiho-nage

Sankyo

Kote gaeshi

Yonkyo

Kaiten-nage

Gokyo

Tenchi-nage

Appendix III: Self-Defence, Weapons and the Law

The ideas, principles and techniques described in this book are all martial in nature and therefore potentially dangerous unless practised in a legitimate school under qualified supervision. Since the nature of all martial arts is to provide skill in self-defence, it is of paramount importance for the practitioner to be aware of the law relating to self-defence in his own country lest he face the prospect of being charged with assault, manslaughter or even murder.

For a successful plea of self-defence under British law, the defendant has to show that he (or another individual) was in immediate physical danger from physical assault and that only reasonable force was used against that assault. Most jury members are likely to assume even the average martial artist to be of super-human expert status, so for the keen practitioner even more caution needs to be taken. That is not to say that the law does not recognize the need for self-defence: Section 3 of the Criminal Law Act 1967 allows 'such force as is reasonable in the circumstances in the prevention of a crime'. What is deemed as 'reasonable' is determined by Common Law, where judgements in individual cases provide interpretation.

A jury has a long time to deliberate on whether or not the force used was reasonable, whereas the victim may have had no more than a few seconds. Consequently, as a martial artist it is your responsibility to think in advance and to train yourself not to over-react, even in a dangerous situation.

Some guidelines when under threat:

- Diffuse the situation.
- Let them say what they want to say.
- Give them what they want, within reason.
- Call attention to others near by.
- Gain help.
- Let it be clear to all present who the aggressor is.
- Be firm and resolute in attitude. Let them know that 'No' means 'No'.
- Effect an escape and withdraw if possible.

Some guidelines when under attack:

- Avoid the attack whenever possible.
- Take a blow or two if necessary; it might satisfy their ego; it will show all present who is starting the trouble.
- Effect an escape and withdraw if possible.
- Restrain and control the aggressor without striking back. Police practise Aikido for this reason. Aikido is an effective controlling art.
- Hit only with half strength, not your full uncontrolled might.

- If you are physically much smaller, more strength might be considered reasonable (for example, in the case of a smaller woman against a larger man).
- Do not continue the attack after the aggressor is under control. This would go beyond what is reasonable.

The over-riding phenomenon in common fights, especially between men, is that often one or both of the 'contestants' are driven more by a perceived injury to their pride than any real threat or danger. Such a situation is magnified by the addition of alcohol. If you are of this type, then it is essential that you learn to reduce your ego (and alcohol intake) to a more controllable level.

Aikido practitioners are often recognized by the 'weapons bag' they carry. While it is fair to say that Aikido wooden swords and knives are perhaps more like replicas of bladed weapons, it is important to note that in the old days in Japan a wooden sword was in itself a formidable weapon. Also, in many countries, including the UK, a wooden staff was used. In this sense, Aikido replica weapons can be regarded as real weapons and appropriate care must be taken both when training and when transporting them to and from the *dojo*. The general rule for transporting them is to keep them covered at all times so that they cannot be readily used. Other than that, in the UK it is illegal to carry an offensive weapon (something made, or adapted for use, as a weapon) for the purposes of self-defence, even if that weapon is not readily recognizable as a weapon (such as a tool or bat). However, if life is endangered by attack, it is within the law to use in your defence something that is available, within the bounds of reason, such as a newspaper, handbag, frying pan or chair.

In conclusion, while the law may appear to be written in stone, Common Law is changeable and ultimate judgement rests upon the subjective mind of keen-eyed jurors. Therefore, it is wise to consider your understanding of the law as part of your system of self-defence, not something that obstructs it.

Glossary of Terms

General
Aikido – 'The Way of Harmony'
aikidoka – person who practises Aikido
tori (*nage*) – the person doing the technique
uke – the person receiving the technique
O Sensei – refers to Ueshiba Morihei, founder of Aikido

In the *dojo*
dojo – training hall
tatami – practice mat
kamiza – seat of the gods
keikogi – practice suit
obi – belt
hakama – traditional Japanese skirt
yudansha – blackbelt (of person)
mudansha/kyu grade – white belt rank
dan – black belt rank
zori – traditional sandals
rei – bow

Posture
kamae – posture (full hip-square posture)
hanmi – half-facing posture
shizen hontai – natural posture
shikko – knee-walking
ayumi-ashi – walking step
tsugi-ashi – shuffling step
tegatana – hand blade
jodan – head level
chudan – mid-level

gedan – lower level
hasso – sword posture, sword pointing straight up
ma-ai – correct distance
zanshin – remaining mind, awareness
hara – centre

Attacks
katate-dori – one hand grabs one hand
ryote-dori – two hands catch two hands
morote-dori – two hands catch one hand
kata-dori – catching the shoulder
mune-dori – catching the chest
hiji-dori – catching the elbow
ushiro ryote-dori – catching two hands to the rear
ushiro katate eri-dori – catching one hand and one lapel from the rear
ushiro kata-dori – rear shoulder grab
ushiro hiji-dori – rear elbow grab
ushiro-dori – catching from behind
shime-waza – strangles and chokes
katate-jime – one-hand strangle
ryote-jime – two-hand strangle
shomen-uchi – frontal head strike
yokomen-uchi – strike to the side of the head
gyaku yokomen-uchi – reverse yokomen-uchi
kesa-giri – diagonal sword strike
tsuki – thrust, or punch
uraken – back-fist
katate-dori shomen-uchi – hand grab and frontal strike

hiji-dori shomen-uchi – elbow grab and frontal strike
do – sword cut to midsection
kata-dori shomen-uchi – shoulder grab and frontal strike
mae-geri – front kick
yoko-geri – side kick
ushiro-geri – rear kick
mawashi-geri – turning kick
atemi – strike(s)

Techniques
kihon – basics
waza – technique
ikkyo – first technique
nikyo – second technique
sankyo – third technique
yonkyo – fourth technique
gokyo – fifth technique
rokkyo – sixth technique
shiho-nage – four (any) direction throw
irimi-nage – entering throw
kote-gaeshi – wrist throw
kaiten-nage – rotation throw
tenchi-nage – Heaven and Earth throw
koshi-nage – hip throw
udekime-nage – extended arm throw
jyuji-nage – cross arm throw
sumi-otoshi – corner drop
hiki-otoshi – elbow drop
ude-garame – arm entanglement
ude-gatame – straight armlock
waki-gatame – side armlock

Methods of practice
suwari-waza – kneeling techniques
hanmi-handachi-waza – half-standing, half-kneeling techniques
tachi-waza – standing techniques
henka-waza – variations
renraku-waza – combination techniques
kaeshi-waza – reversal techniques
koryu-no-kata – old sets of techniques
ninin-dori – two attackers on to one
tanin-dori – multiple attackers

randori – free practice
jiyu-waza – free practice
keisaku – beat training
shiai – contest
misogi – spiritual cleansing
ki-no-nagare – flowing practice

Major principles
mae-ukemi – front break-fall
ushiro-ukemi – rear break-fall
tenkan-ho – turning exercise
taisabaki – body turning
torifune – rowing exercise
kokyu-ho – breath exercise
kokyu-ryoku – breath power
kokyu-nage – breath throw
kuzushi – breaking balance
tsukuri – making technique
suki – gap
happo – eight directions
aiki – feeling of liquid flow
ki – life energy
kiai – focused shout
irimi (*omote*) – entering
tenkan (*ura*) – turning
sokumen – side entry
zanshin – remaining mind/being alert

Weapons
bokken – wooden sword
jo – staff
tanto – knife
tsuba – blade guard
ai-uchi – both striking at the same time
ai-nuke – both escaping at the same time
Aiki-ken – Aikido sword training
kama – sickle, scythe

Major styles mentioned
Aikikai Aikido (Ueshiba Morihei)
Yoshinkan Aikido (Shioda Gozo)
Iwama Aikido (Saito Morihiro)
Shodokan Aikido (Tomiki Kenji)
Takeda-ryu So Budo (Nakamura Hisashi)

Ki Aikido (Tohei Koichi)
Judo (Kano Jigoro)
Kyushindo (Abe Kenshiro)
Jujutsu (various styles)
Daito Ryu (Takeda Sokatu)
Jukendo – Japanese bayonet art
Jodo – Japanese stick art
Kenjutsu – Japanese sword art
Miyamoto Musashi (famous swordsman)
Taichichuan – a Chinese art

Budo – martial way
Zen – Japanese sect of Buddhism

Other terms
shu-ha-ri – studying, thinking for yourself,
    forming your own school
yin/yang – negative/positive duality
Shodan – first grade black belt
mokuso – silent thought
satori – enlightenment

Index